INSIDE
ROBOTICS

A practical guide to building and operating robots safely

James Cooper

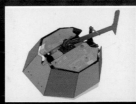

Rosen
YA
New York

Contents

This edition published in 2019 by:
The Rosen Publishing Group, Inc.
29 East 21st Street
New York, NY 10010

Additional end matter copyright © 2019 by The Rosen
Publishing Group, Inc.

Cataloging-in-Publication Data
Names: Cooper, James.
Title: Inside robotics / James Cooper.
Description: New York : Rosen YA, 2019. | Series: The
geek's guide to computer science | Includes glossary
and index.
Identifiers: LCCN ISBN 9781508185819 (pbk.) |
ISBN 9781508185802 (library bound)
Subjects: LCSH: Robots—Design and construction—
Juvenile literature. | Robotics—Juvenile literature.
Classification: LCC TJ211.2 C667 2019 |
DDC 629.8'92--dc23

Manufactured in the United States of America

Originally published in English by Haynes Publishing
under the title: Build Your Own Robot manual © James
Cooper 2017

Cover: 3alexd/E+/Getty Images

The *Robot Wars* story

Types of robot and their applications

Design and development of a House Robot

The anatomy of a House Robot

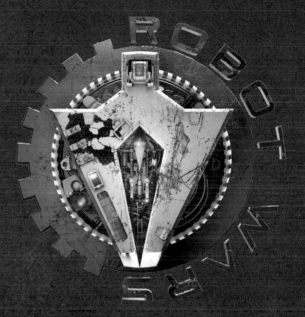

Building a robot safely

Build your own robot

How to win Robot Wars

Appendices

1

The *Robot* *Wars* story

Robot Wars is the hugely successful television series produced by Mentorn for MTV Networks in the United States and for the BBC and Channel 5 in the United Kingdom.

More than 150 programs were produced between 1998 and 2003, and the show was then revived by Mentorn, SJP Media and the BBC in 2016 and is now bigger and better than ever.

Robot Wars is a robot combat competition involving teams of "roboteers" who design and build fighting robots and then operate them in battles with other contestants' robots, through a series of rounds until a champion is crowned! They fight in a specially built arena, filled with hazards such as the flame pit and surrounded

by bullet-proof polycarbonate screens to keep the roboteers and the audience safe from injury by flying pieces of robot.

And, as well as the contestants' robots, there are of course the terrifying House Robots. Huge and deadly fighting machines, the House Robots can weigh into the battles when called upon, destroying competitors' robots with their weaponry, so the contestants need to keep clear of Sir Killalot, Shunt, Matilda and Dead Metal, or they risk total destruction.

Robot Wars programs have been shown all around the world, from Germany to Thailand and from India to Australia. They have created a worldwide fanbase and inspired robot-building enthusiasts everywhere.

Robot Wars history

⬇ **The original ad Marc Thorpe placed in the paper to advertise his new idea.**

But how did this spectacular TV series come to our television screens? The story goes back to San Francisco in the 1990s and an American special-effects engineer.

Robot Wars started life as a live event and was the brainchild of Marc Thorpe, a San Francisco-based artist/designer/engineer. Marc decided to stage a live robot combat competition with some Hollywood special effects designers he knew, and other robot enthusiasts.

Marc says: "Now I had to raise money. So I entered into an agreement with Profile Records and Steve Plotnicki" and the first annual *Robot Wars* event then took place in August 1994 in San Francisco, California.

"Of the 1,200 people who attended, 178 were press from around the world!" says Marc. "The first event was a raging success. The contestants were a wonderful mix of imagination, skill, humor and just plain fun. There were no wedge robots and only one spinner, Charley Tilford's South Bay Mauler. He won the final melée event. In the second year, 1995, people knew what to do. Out of nowhere came La Machine, the first wedge, which was a middleweight that ended up dominating the whole field of competitors, including the heavyweights. That event was a screaming success as well."

Three further *Robot Wars* events took place

➔➔ **The original *Wired* magazine interview with *Robot Wars* founder Marc Thorpe.**

Here's an old movie plot: To minimize the human impact of war, the nations of the world agree to have robots do the fighting. Of course, one side is bound to not like the outcome ("It wuz fixed…we wuz robbed") and so may start a war over that.

The plot may be fiction, but the robot battle is real. Marc Thorpe is waging the first "Robot Wars" on August 20 and 21, 1994 at Fort Mason in San Francisco. "I don't feel uncomfortable about destruction," says Thorpe. "Promoting combat between robots instead of people is a healthy alternative. That it's aggressive, combative, and survival-oriented gives it a kind of energy that professional football has."

Thorpe has launched a PR blitz for "Robot Wars," inviting mad mechanics, technophiles, and movie special-effects teams to build radio-controlled robots designed to rip, punch, and impale each other to scrap metal and frayed rubber while onlookers scream like ancient Romans at the Colosseum. And if mere robot opponents aren't enough, hydraulic shears and presses placed within the 40-by-60-foot arena will chomp, stomp, and sayonara any dull-witted robot who happens to linger too long in the wrong place.

There are three contests: one-on-one survival of the fittest, a mob scene, and the neatest, where your bot has to escort a defenseless dronebot across the arena. The three weight classes were set up so your delicate, 25-pound, eighteen-legged centipede doesn't have to face a 100-pound crusher with a snorting chainsaw for a beak. And it's not quite "anything goes" – no explosives, corrosives, fire breathing dragons, or "untethered projectiles" (guns); no radio jamming or interfering with the other human operators allowed. Entry fees per robot are US$50 for individuals and $500 for corporations. (It's a business expense: Put your logos where the TV cameras can see them.)

For details and an entry form e-mail robotwars@aol.com, or phone +1 (415) 453 6305.
– Jef Raskin

Robot War Games

in America, and in 1995, Mentorn created a television format based on the *Robot Wars* concept after they had learned of the events in San Fransisco.

Mentorn partnered with Profile Records to stage a live event in a warehouse opposite BBC Television Centre in London. They hired Derek Foxwell to build 3 combat robots, 2 of which were named The Mouse and Grunt (who would eventually take part in the first UK series

of *Robot Wars),* and they flew into London three American robots – Thor, La Machine and The Master – all of which were veterans of the original American competition.

Mentorn invited the BBC2 Controller, Michael Jackson, to the event so they could persuade him it would make a great TV show. And it worked! Soon there was a BBC series underway and *Robot Wars* was about to conquer the World!

The evolution of the competitor robots

Original TV Series

The first series of *Robot Wars* on the BBC had a more rustic, scrapyard feel.

Teams used whatever they had to build their robots. One used a metal road sign, while others repurposed old scooters. It really was an incredible achievement by 36 teams to produce those brilliant working robots in time for filming. They may not have been the hugely complex machines we see today, but they were groundbreaking for their time. Many weren't built to take advantage of the contest's full weight limit, some weighing in at less than half the maximum weight allowed. But with each

subsequent series an incredible amount of experience was gained and the robots evolved.

By Series 2, the legendary Razer made its debut, using new technologies, and the incredible power of hydraulics was revealed for all to see. It also showed that a robot didn't have to look like it came from a scrap pile. Razer was the first "art bot" – a robot with real character and beauty.

Series 3 saw another big leap in the quality and competitiveness of robots, along with new designs that showed signs of great promise. Pneumatic systems had advanced and Chaos 2 became famous for its highly effective flipper

→ **The very first *Robot Wars* event – The Master built by Mark Setrakian vs The Beetle built by Caleb Cheung. Both roboteers would go on to be world leaders in their fields. Setrakian created the *Robot Fighting League* TV show while Cheung created toys such as the Furby.**

weapon. We also saw the birth of Hypnodisc – the first robot to demonstrate how flywheels could store huge amounts of kinetic energy, causing devastating levels of damage.

In Series 4 and 5, fan-favorite robots became legends as they honed their designs during periods of fantastic engineering development. Robots were more precisely built. It became an arms race to try to be the lowest to the floor, making the robots' weapons even more effective. The weight limit was also increased, and the machines took another big step, becoming even more reliable and effective. Robots broke down less frequently. Defeat was more likely to be at the hands of a competitor than a faulty motor during Series 5, and Razer finally became the UK champion with a very effective weapon, but an even more effective drive system, paving the way for teams to focus on both design and driving skills.

Series 6 and 7 saw the rise of Tornado and Storm 2, again highlighting the importance of drive systems and driver skills, using brute force and speed to make combat as much about the driving as the weapons. We also saw a big development in armor materials, and the effectiveness of flywheels being developed by Supanova and Typhoon 2.

↑ The original house robots were much smaller than today's. This is the original Sir Killalot.

← Razer, Series 2.

↓ Tornado, Series 6.

↑ The Series 4 House Robots – Dead Metal, Matilda, Sir Killalot, Refbot, Sergeant Bash and Shunt.

Robot Wars Revival 2016

In 2016, the BBC, together with production company Mentorn Scotland and SJP Media, heralded the beginning of a new *Robot Wars* era. Following a hiatus of more than a decade since full combat had been shown on screens in the UK. Machines from the past had to prepare for taking on the new generation of big spinners. The weight increase to 243 pounds (110 kg) allowed teams to modify existing robots and build new machines to take advantage of the new rules. The series saw big technological advances throughout. RC radio gear was now far more reliable meaning teams didn't just "lose signal." The biggest advancement was the use of lithium batteries, which gave teams far more power in a lightweight package, saving crucial weight which could be used for armor or weaponry.

Though robots competing in Series 9 the previous year had witnessed many reliability issues occur, their teams — including those handing out damage as well as those receiving it – were unprepared for the intense combat of the new age. Machines like Carbide and Ironside were able to dispense huge hits on their opponents and yet survive the impacts themselves. Teams consequently learned a great deal about armor mounting and materials as the impacts increased in energy. This series also saw a couple of teams start to implement brushless motors. However, despite showing great potential they needed more development time.

Prior to Series 10, there was a concern about the imbalance in the arena due to the power of the big spinners. This led to a rule change that allowed teams to add entanglement devices to tackle the spinners. The series therefore saw a large leap in creativity as teams took advantage of this rule

↑ Hypnodisc in action.　　↓ The crowd.

→ Storm 2.

← **Series 8 champions Apollo prepared for battle.**

change. Surprisingly, it was the "odd" robots you wouldn't have thought posed much of a threat that started to highlight new ways of winning, with eccentric innovations, contrary to the theory that you needed a big spinner or a flipper to be successful. Instead, thinking outside the box saw many teams achieve well-deserved surprise victories over the established top dogs. Big Nipper and Magnetar also showed glimpses of the future potential of brushless-motor systems. Although still not at their full potential, they are likely to be the next big technological innovation in *Robot Wars.*

←↓ **Eruption and Aftershock going head to head.**

← Sir Killalot toasts his victim on the Flame Pit.

Robot Wars – the battle

What you can and can't build

There are a number of rules that competitors must adhere to. At the beginning of every *Robot Wars* event the technical team implement checks. All teams must successfully complete their Technical Check before they can be signed off as ready for battle.

To pass this, a detailed inspection of each competitor's robot – both inside and out – is completed, ensuring that it fully complies with all *Robot Wars* build, health and safety rules. During these checks the teams must also pass a functionality test to ensure their robot performs correctly inside the test arena. If a robot has suffered severe damage during the competition, it may need to go through another Technical Check before it is permitted to continue battling.

Some of the rules are for safety reasons and some are for technical reasons, to ensure the robots have been built to a suitable standard for safe and fair competition while still allowing teams diversity and creativity when designing and building their robots. You'll find the Build Rules in the Appendices, however it's worth examining the principal rules here regarding what teams can and cannot do.

Firstly, the most fundamental rule in *Robot Wars* is the weight limit. Set at 243 pounds (110 kg) for standard wheeled robots, this is the fundamental limiter that stops teams entering indestructible tanks or giant robots with ten weapons attached. There *are* extra weight bonuses available if you create an interesting robot with a unique drive system, such as a shuffler or walker. However, the

↓ The test arena, where all robots must pass strict safety checks.

weight limit creates a "level playing field," while still giving teams the potential to create incredibly powerful robots without becoming too heavy, cumbersome or expensive.

The next big rule is that which governs weapon restrictions. Naturally, there are many banned weapons that teams aren't permitted to use, such as liquids and electricity. These are banned not only for health and safety reasons, but also because they tend not to cause visible damage that the audience at home can actually see. Only kinetic-energy weapons – *ie* objects or weapons that move – are permitted.

The arena, how it works and the hazards

The *Robot Wars* arena itself is a huge feat of engineering. The enormous structure weighs in at over 55 tons (50 t) and is the only environment safe enough to contain these immense fighting robots. It's a semi-permanent structure that's currently housed in a huge warehouse in Glasgow containing three mighty 220-ton (200 t) cranes used to raise and lower the entire roof of the arena!

The arena comprises three sections. The outer arena is a huge sealed structure made from custom steel frames that retain the polycarbonate/bulletproof screens. These screens are especially designed and rigorously tested to ensure high-speed debris and robots can't escape the arena. Large fragments of robot can often be heard ricocheting off the walls and roof at high velocity. You can only hear the fastest of these impacts, as the debris is moving too fast to be seen. On three sides of the arena, a catwalk leads from a tunnel in the audience seating to a pair of ominous-looking 13 foot (4 m) tall doors, through which the teams bring their machines to commence battle. The catwalks extend over the trench that connects to the inner arena.

The inner arena is where the action takes place in the combat area. Although this space may look huge, there's no place to hide when all the hazards, House Robots and opponents are in there with you! This inner arena is raised about 3.3 feet (1 m) off the ground level and has a floor made from sheet steel to ensure it can take impacts from the robots during battle. The walls are also made from steel, 3 feet (0.9 m) tall and reinforced with large steel I-beams. For the most part these walls are extended to 6.6 feet (2 m) tall with polycarbonate, to stop robots being flipped out too easily.

Where the catwalks connect to the inner arena there is a hydraulic wall section that is lowered and raised to allow robots to enter the arena before battle. Once the robots are loaded, armed and ready for battle, the teams exit the arena via the catwalks and head up to

→ The *Robot Wars* arena.

the Roboteer Control Booths. These booths are raised 8.2 feet (2.5 m) in the air to provide the teams with the best possible vantage point for driving their robots. The raised area also gives the audience the best possible view of the roboteers as they prepare for battle!

Of course, the *Robot Wars* arena wouldn't be an arena without its hazards! The inner arena contains five large hazards that the teams may use to their advantage at any time.

Firstly, there are the Spikes, five CO_2-powered metal points that shoot up at random with such force that they can flip robots over and cause serious damage to their vulnerable underbelly.

The next hazard is the Flame Pit. The heat from these bursts of flame can melt soft tires and internal wiring, so it's vital to escape the flames as soon as you can in order to avoid major internal damage.

Then there's the Floor Flipper, which uses high-pressure CO_2 to launch any robot that inadvertently strays over its target panel.

Another popular hazard is the CPZs – the Corner Patrol Zones. These marked-off areas are where the House Robots lurk, so you enter them at your peril. The House Robots take no prisoners, so if you're pushed or accidentally drive into a CPZ you have an almighty opponent to escape from!

Finally there's the infamous Pit, which spells the end for any robot that falls into it. It can be the cruellest hazard of all if, when it drops, you happen to be in the wrong place at the wrong time.

However, it can also be a saving grace if a hard-pressed team manages to force its opponent into it. The Pit is activated using the "Pit Tire."

↑ **Inside the arena.**

↓ **Inside the drivers' booth.**

↑ The punishing Spike Pit.

➔ The Flame Pit.

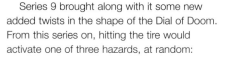

↘ The Floor Flipper ready for action.

↓ Dead Metal guards his CPZ.

Series 9 brought along with it some new added twists in the shape of the Dial of Doom. From this series on, hitting the tire would activate one of three hazards, at random:

- ■ The Pit floor drops, or if hit a second time rises back up.
- ■ This is a new hazard called The Fog of War. The arena fills with dense fog for ten seconds, disorientating the competitors and leaving them at the mercy of the House Robots who lurk undetected in the Fog.
- ■ The third hazard is Rogue House Robot. Any

or all of the House Robots is free to attack any or all of the competitors for a period of 10 seconds. The perfect way to unsettle a competitor, but be careful that you don't become the unwilling victim of a ruthless House Robot.

The battle rules and the judging criteria

In each round of a Robot Wars competition, the robots engage in a timed battle, with the winners decided by either a knockout or, if the time runs out with no clear winner, a judge's decision made

by a panel of three expert judges.

There are three ways to win by a knockout:

- Flipping an opponent out of the arena into the surrounding trench.
- Maneuvering your opponent into the Pit hazard inside the arena.
- Immobilizing your opponent for ten seconds through extensive damage or if your opponent breaks down and is therefore unable to continue.

In the event that a battle goes to a Judges' decision, they will be awarding a win based on the following three criteria:

- **Damage** – causing clear damage to an opponent both visually and internally.
- **Aggression** – a robot consistently taking the battle to its opponents.
- **Control** – demonstrating good driving skills and weapon accuracy throughout the battle.

Each category will be scored from 1 to 5 points, the scores being weighted to reflect their importance as follows:

Aggression – 3 points
Damage – 2 points
Control – 1 point.

This will result in an overall score, and the robot with the highest overall score wins the battle.

↑ The Dial of Doom. Swing left for the pit, center to activate Fog of War and right to unleash the House Robots.

← TERRORHURTZ claims victory by dumping Carbide down the Pit.

↓ Shunt chasing down victim Carbide during Rogue House Robot.

2

Types of robot and their applications

What does the term robot mean?

So, what *is* a robot? When we think of robots, humanoid machines from science fiction movies immediately spring to mind. Androids doing chores in futuristic homes and cyborgs trying to take over the world in epic battles against humanity. In reality, however, there are many different types of robot, most of which don't take on a human form at all. In fact the term "robot" simply means a machine that can carry out one or more tasks automatically. The word itself comes from *robota*, the Latin word for "servitude," and was first coined in 1920 by writer Karel Capek and his brother Joseph when describing artificial characters in their plays.

Where do robots come from?

The first ever robot is widely believed to have been a mechanical bird made in the 4th century BC by Greek mathematician Archytas of Tarentum. The Pigeon, as he called it, was made of wood and flapped its wings, which were powered by steam. Development of robots began to accelerate during the Renaissance, when, in 1495, Leonardo da Vinci designed one of the first recorded humanoid robots. One of his notebooks, rediscovered in the 1950s, detailed a complex mechanical knight that could stand, sit, wave its arms and move its head, controlled by a complex series of pulleys and cables.

With each new development in technology engineers were able to create ever more complex and intricate machines. In the 18th century, Japanese astronomer and inventor Hanzo Hosokawa created one of the first automated tea-serving dolls. Karakuri, as it was known, stood approximately 10 inches (26 cm) tall and was able to carry out incredibly complex operations and tasks. Despite batteries being hard to come by in the 18th century, Hanzo used an intricate system of gears and springs to power the robot. Karakuri was able to carry a cup of tea on a tray, bow its head and even serve the tea. Once the cup was empty, the doll would turn and depart.

Today, robots interact with our everyday lives and are shaping the world around us. Domestic robots are everywhere, designed for our convenience and to make our lives easier. There are robots that clean our floors and mow our lawns, and soon there will be advanced robots that can drive us to work by combining complex software with state-of-the-art sensors to detect the roads and hazards along the way. By 2019 it's expected there will be 31 million household robots worldwide!

Robots are also used to a great extent in industry, to increase efficiency in factory production lines. These robots are designed for speed and accuracy, to enable manufacturers to create their goods much faster and to a higher standard than humans could achieve. According to *Executive Summary World Robotics 2016*, the automobile industry employs 38% of all industrial robots, used to speed up the assembly of vehicles. Robots don't have to be physical machines, though. Companies have also developed virtual robots called 'bots', which are software programs that can perform automated tasks. A great example of this would be a video game bot, an in-game computer-controlled opponent that analyzes your every move and adapts its own strategies accordingly.

⬇ **A robot delivers food to customers in a Chinese restaurant.** *(Getty Images)*

How TV shaped the way we see robots

Television and film has certainly influenced the way we see robots, and media robots have inspired us for generations. Iconic machines such as C-3PO and the Terminator have brought highly advanced humanoid robots to life for us, given us a glimpse into the future and instilled the belief that such advanced machines may one day walk alongside us. However, such robots – if they were real – are far more advanced than any humanoid robots we can produce today. But we're getting much closer. Boston Dynamics, an advanced robotics company in the United States, was originally set up to develop the first robots that could run and move like animals. Their first ground-breaking machine was Big Dog, a quadrupedal robot created in 2005.

Big Dog was designed to be an all-terrain pack mule that would accompany soldiers, and use its four legs to carry up to 330 pounds (150 kg) at 4 miles (6 km) per hour. Today Boston Dynamics combine cutting-edge engineering with perception and intelligence software to create some of the most agile robots in the world. Their latest robots, Atlas and Handle, are the closest things to seeing

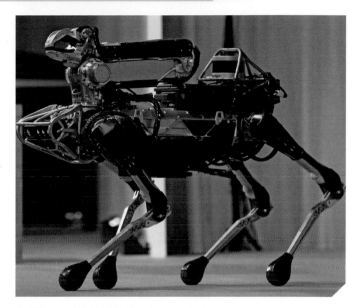

C-3PO in real life! Yet it's the simpler robots, like R2D2 and the Daleks (though the latter are androids), that really capture our imaginations. The ability of such simple-looking mechanisms to portray heroism and villainy makes them some of the most loved robots in media history.

↑ One of the latest four-legged robot developments from Boston Dynamics – Spot Mini.
(Getty Images)

Are the *Robot Wars* robots actually robots?

Are the robots on *Robot Wars* actually robots? There are legitimate points on both sides of this argument, especially given the loose definition of what a robot actually is. Some people say a robot must have some form of autonomy or self-sufficiency, and some say they're simply remote-controlled vehicles. If we think about a robot as being something that carries out one or more tasks automatically, a remote-controlled vehicle differs from an industrial robot arm only in that, for the vehicle, its commands are decided and sent live via a remote-control device whereas the robotic arm tends to have its commands pre-programmed in a computer.

A robot arm may have extra sensors to detect overloading, or to ensure that it's in the correct position before releasing a component on a production line, and as such it's detecting its environment and making simple decisions to react to it. *Robot Wars* robots have similar functionality. If the robot has extra load, and is therefore drawing more current, the motor controllers may be able to detect this and limit the power going to the motors to ensure components aren't damaged. Or if the on-board batteries are getting too low it may shut down the robot in order to preserve them. Besides, if you were to control a robot arm via a joystick it wouldn't suddenly *not* be a robot any more. Either way, a robot in both of these instances is simply a machine made up of motors, motor controllers and some form of input device.

3

Design and development of a House Robot

Character-led design

The House Robots' designs are solely led by their personalities, while also ensuring the specification of their new components and armor ensures their legendary status.

Each of the House Robots has an individual identity, so it is critical to fully understand each one.

Matilda, has a resilient attitude, but a bad temper. During the finals of the infamous Southern Annihilator battle she suffered at the hands of Razer. Matilda had been pushed around more and more during the original *Robot Wars*, as the competitor robots steadily

↓ The original House Robots in storage.

grew in strength and power. We needed to put those days behind us. Matilda would return with a battle-hardened attitude, angry and ready to take on any robot that strayed into her CPZ (Corner Patrol Zone). Matilda had a grudge to settle!

Shunt is the workhorse of *Robot Wars*. A stoic, super-sized, super-powerful House Robot, always ready to rumble. He dominates the *Robot Wars* arena with his no-nonsense, brute-force approach, and remains the ultimate spinner killer. Shunt is often the default House Robot as he is

designed to be able to take on all competitor weapon types.

Dead Metal evolved to become a futuristic machine, she is a scorpion-like robot-killer with a blade that can chew into the toughest of advanced armors.

Sir Killalot, the king of the House Robots, has always had an intimidating presence in the arena. Muscular, sharp and high-tech, but most importantly of all he casts a shadow over his opponents. With his new evolved power, Sir Killalot was the most formidable robot to return to the *Robot Wars* arena. In his latest form, the top section of the helmet has been removed to reveal Sir Killalot himself – a sinister, robotic, skeletal creature from another world!

↑ **Top-secret mood boards and sketches for the new House Robots.**

← **Creating the molds for the newly evolved Matilda head.**

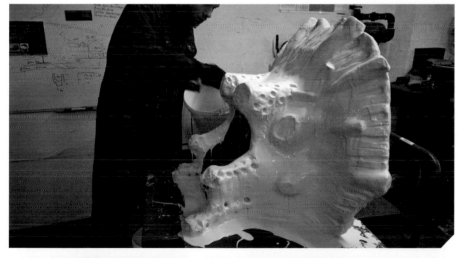

← **The new-style Dead Metal coming together. More modern, more spikes and more aggressive.**

Why the House Robots had to beef up

Ever since the early series of *Robot Wars*, groups of amateur builders hosted their own fighting-robot events. Teams would gather on a regular basis to battle their homemade machines in front of local audiences. Over this time these teams developed, perfected and enhanced their machines creating tougher robots with vastly more experienced drivers. The House Robots needed to evolve to maintain their place in the hierarchy. There was one caveat, though. Prior to the latest series, there wasn't an arena safe enough to run the big destructive spinner robots. These robots require much higher levels of safety when it comes to arenas, due to the high velocity of debris generated by big impacts.

At that time, many of the most successful robots were the big flippers. However, with the news that *Robot Wars* would return with the toughest fighting arena in the World, teams

→ **Testing a spinning weapon rig to evaluate the impacts on different materials.**

↓ **Series 9 champion Carbide, complete with spare spinners. Note the *Robot Wars* trophy on the workbench.**

began to look to the big American spinners for inspiration. Knowing that the House Robots would now have to take on the very best machines from around the world without ever breaking down, they needed to evolve.

So, what's the difference between today's competitors and some of the best robots from the original series? Let's take a look at some of the iconic legends and see how they compare now.

Firstly, Razer, arguably the most famous crusher robot of all time. A double world champion and one of the most successful fighting robots ever built, its predatory animal-style hydraulic pincer had three tons of crushing power, and was formidable in the original series. Few robots left the arena without Razer's signature crusher holes in them. Incredible in its day.

Razer had literally half the crushing force of one of the best modern crushers, Tiberius. A meticulously designed hydraulic robot, Tiberius produces 6.6 tons (6 t) of force at the tip of the crushing claw that twists and bends almost all its robot competitors!

Chaos 2 – double *Robot Wars* champion and famous for flipping its opponents out of the arena with ease – could toss its opponents more than 3 feet (1 m) in the air. But today's top flippers – Eruption, Apollo and Rapid – can easily launch robots 6 feet (2 m) in the air, hence the new arena walls had to be significantly raised compared to the original arena. Robots would have been flying out in a matter of seconds!

Finally, let's look at the legendary Hypnodisc, the robot every team feared. Very few robots left the arena in one piece once Hypnodisc was up to speed, which earned the team its legendary status as one of the fan favorites of the original series of *Robot Wars.* Although very effective in its day, Hypnodisc's weapon is actually quite ineffective against the modern armor of today's competitors. When you compare Hypnodisc to Series 9 champion Carbide, there's a huge difference in power. Team Carbide estimate that their modern spinner weapon has 60kJ of energy – six times the energy of Hypnodisc!

The technology of the House Robots

Robot Wars contestants have to abide by a strict set of rules that limit certain factors for the teams. The most limiting rule is the maximum weight limit. Similar to boxing, the machines entered for *Robot Wars* often choose to be as heavy as possible, to ensure that they can accommodate the biggest weapons possible, the best armor, and the highest-powered motors.

You might think that building a robot to half the permissible weight to make it more nimble and quicker might be an advantage, but, again just like boxing, if an opponent twice its size came into the arena it would make easy pickings of a lighter machine. So the maximum weight influences the size robots can be, the amount of power they can use for the weaponry and the thickness of the armor they can carry.

Fortunately, the House Robots aren't governed by these rules. For them there's no weight limit, giving them a huge advantage. They can be as big, as powerful and as strong as they need to be. Matilda, Shunt and Dead Metal weigh in at more than three times the competitors' maximum limit – close to 770 pounds (350 kg) each. They have far more powerful drive motors than competitors could hope for. Their weapons are in another league too, and the sheer size of the House Robots casts a shadow over the teams' machines, to ensure they know who's the boss. Sir Killalot

← James working on one of Sir Killalot's drive pods. Each one weighs more than the maximum weight limit of *Robot Wars* competitors.

weighs in at an incredible 1,634 pounds (741 kg), almost seven times the weight of the competitor robots. It really shows when he's in the arena. Nobody can push Sir Killalot around.

As there's no weight limit for the House Robots, there's no need to be so conscious of weight-savings. However, there are other limitations that had to be considered. Firstly, despite not having a weight limit, the House Robots still needed to be as compact and efficient as possible, to ensure they were fast and agile despite their size and weight. After all, they wouldn't be very useful if they were ponderous giants that competitors' robots could run rings around. They also needed to fit through the arena doors!

← Dead Metal's jaws are big enough to engulf the entire old Dead Metal.

↑ The House Robots.

→ Shunt's newly formed bucket being welded up.

↓ Shunt ready for action!

Shunt

Weight – 720 pounds (327 kg)

Weapons – A bulldozer bucket with 770-pound (350 kg) lifting power, which is enough to launch competitors on to their backs to expose their vulnerable underbelly. Also a titanium axe that fires in less than quarter of a second and can penetrate some of the toughest armors around.

Armor – Hardox, a very tough wear-plate steel.

Shunt is the *Robot Wars* bruiser, who deals with competitors by brute force alone. Designed to take on the deadliest of spinners, Shunt's bulldozer bucket tips over its victims so that his axe can fire at their underbelly. Shunt has caused some serious damage throughout the new era of *Robot Wars*, most notably immobilizing Draven with a single hit through the titanium armor. He also caused a blaze by chopping straight through the batteries of Chopalot.

Being a robust, mean machine, the new incarnation of Shunt required a more industrial approach than the other House Robots. Shunt has a bulldozer bucket made of from very wear-resistant steel necessary to take big hits from the latest big spinner robots. The curved scoop required a hydraulic press providing an incredible 55 tons (50 t) of force.

→ Shunt takes on PP3D.

Dead Metal

Weight – 756 pounds (343 kg)
Weapons – A saw blade at 211 miles (340 km) per hour mounted in Dead Metal's retracting head. Jaws have 660 pounds (300 kg) of gripping force and can engulf multiple competitors within her 5 foot (1.5 m) jaw width.
Armor – Tubular steel.

Dead Metal is a futuristic alien robot. She's always on the hunt and loves circling next to the Fire Pit. Once she's got hold of her victim in those powerful arms, there's no escape from the saw! Dead Metal's weapon is unique, in that it's designed to melt through armor rather than cut. This means even the toughest robots will suffer damage.

Dead Metal is a creature as much as a machine. The body is made from various sized tubes handcrafted to give her an organic grown feel that's not perfectly symmetrical. During the finals of Series 9, her jaws were damaged by the destructive vertical spinner of Aftershock, so for Series 10 she was given a new set of super-tough pincers that hardly sustained a scratch throughout Series 10.

→ **Dead Metal guarding the CPZ.**

↓ **Dead Metal lurking.**

↘ **Dead Metal takes a bite out of Foxic.**

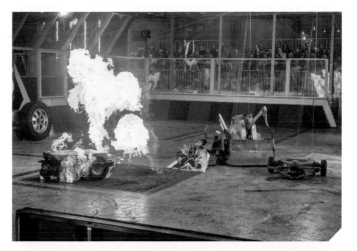

↑ Matilda backstage ready to wreak havoc.

← Matilda chaos!

Matilda

Weight – 770 pounds (350 kg)
Weapons – Tusks that have 1.7 tons (1.5 t) of lifting force, plus a rear flywheel.
Armor – Fiberglass and Kevlar composite.

Matilda is back! Her armor may not be the strongest, but what she lacks in robustness she more than makes up for with weaponry. Now battle-hardened, with huge launching tusks and the most destructive of all the House Robots' arsenal, a savage rear flywheel. During Series 9 this flywheel launched Nuts 2 out of the arena right from Matilda's own CPZ – one of the biggest impacts to date.

Her unique spines look very sharp, but are actually made of a soft material. This helps with their durability in the arena. One big evolution from the original series is the flipping tusks. The whole head now kicks up when the flipper is fired, changing the geometry of the flipper and making it far more effective.

← Matilda tears the side off Thor.

Sir Killalot

Weight – 1,634 pounds (741 kg)
Weapons – 14-ton (12.7 t) hydraulic crushing jaw and 661-pound (300 kg) lifting lance.
Armour – Armox military grade wear-plate steel.

Sir Killalot is the undisputed king of the *Robot Wars* arena. Weighing more than double the other House Robots and seven times as much as competitor robots. Robots have tried to take on Sir Killalot, but all have failed. During the grand finals of Series 9, the new champion Carbide tried to take out the House Robots after a ceasefire was called, but was decisively dealt with by Shunt and Sir Killalot in a shower of sparks! More recently, in an epic ten-way redemption melee, there was an agreement between all the teams to gang up on Sir Killalot. However, on "Activate," TERRORHURTZ and Thor were the only teams brave enough to try, and both were mercilessly dispatched.

The new Sir Killalot is a real metal monster, required to take on the strongest competitors while being nimble enough to catch them. Therefore, his custom-made high-power track system was designed and made specifically for him.

Sir Killalot is refined and further improved every series. Following Series 8, his hydraulic system was upgraded with 50% more power and much finer control. He also had a new pair of specially designed claws to help snag his victims! This had a huge impact helping him to capture and crush his unsuspecting competitors.

Sir Killalot isn't there just to destroy robots, but also plays a critical safety role. For instance, if a competitor robot's spinning weapon was jammed on at full speed, using his hydraulic claw, which can be controlled very accurately and precisely, Sir Killalot would be capable of picking up the errant robot and stopping the spinner on the arena side wall or floor to enable the robot to be safely disarmed.

⬆ **Sir Killalot.**

⬇ **Sir Killalot keeps order during the 2016 Christmas celebrity special.**

⬅ **Sir Killalot at the Robo Challenge workshop getting prepared for Series 10.**

4

The anatomy of a House Robot

Different types of chassis

One of the key things to consider when building a House Robot, or any robot for that matter, is the chassis. The chassis holds together all the important elements of a robot, such as the drive wheels, the weapons, the batteries and everything else you have to squeeze into a robot to make it work. That's why it's so important to choose the right sort of chassis.

The three main chassis types commonly met with in *Robot Wars* – monocoque, tubular and bulkhead, each of which has its own advantages and disadvantages.

Monocoque chassis

The monocoque chassis is one of the most common in the newer series of *Robot Wars*. It's effectively a chassis that uses its outer armor as one large shell in which everything else sits.

↓ Apollo's Hardox chassis laid out ready to assemble.

This approach has been used very successfully by Series 8 champions Apollo and Series 9 champions Carbide.

One of the key benefits of monocoque chassis, and the reason they've become so popular, is the speed and ease with which they can be built. With laser and plasma cutting becoming much more affordable, monocoque chassis can be designed, sent to a laser cutting company and cut out the very next day very cheaply. It's almost a flat-pack robot that needs only to be welded together!

The downside of this type, however, is that the chassis is also the armor. This means that it's the only thing that's taking all the energy from big hits, and therefore needs to be designed very carefully to ensure there's sufficient strength in all the right areas. Apollo's chassis thickness increases from 0.1-inch (3 mm) Hardox elsewhere to 0.2-inch (6 mm) Hardox on the front, where it takes most of the impacts. If a monocoque robot's armor is twisted by a big impact, that's the chassis bent, and your robot's performance will suffer, especially if it's a four-wheel-drive robot, where all the wheels need to contact the floor evenly.

In addition, due to monocoque chassis usually being cut from sheet metal, it's often very difficult to make them look visually exciting. Consequently their character tends to depend on the creativity of their paintwork.

Tubular chassis

The tubular chassis used to be one of the most popular in the early days of *Robot Wars*, when CNC laser cutting was out of most teams' price range. This type of chassis was made famous by championship-winning robots such as Tornado and Storm 2.

Often made from cheap and readily available steel tube, a tubular chassis can be quickly created in anyone's garage with a hacksaw and a welder. Although this method is now most commonly seen in robots built on a budget, if they're done properly they can nevertheless prove worthy of their place in the arena.

A tubular chassis allows robot builders more freedom with armor, allowing interchangeable

panels to be bolted on and off and the attachment of sculpted fiberglass shells, such as those used on Terror-Turtle and Megamouse. It also allows armor to easily be rubber mounted for defense against spinners, and enables the components of awkward-shaped robots to be mounted in unconventional positions more easily, without using up critical weight and cost in materials.

The downside to a tubular chassis is that it can be very easily damaged if the armor isn't designed well enough to take big hits, as these forces can be transmitted directly through the armor and into the thinner and weaker tubes, causing welds to break or tubes to deform.

Central or major bulkheads

One of the more complex and stronger chassis is made using main bulkheads of either sheet steel or thick aluminium. These tend to be thick, strong bulkheads that take most of the force of the robot's weapon and hold the internal components together. Rapid, TERRORHURTZ and Sabretooth use very similar methods successfully.

Solid bulkheads allow the weapon and drive systems to be mounted together in a very lightweight yet strong chassis that allows great flexibility in choice of armor, as this doesn't tend to dictate the overall shape of the robot.

← Sabretooth's internal bulkheads without armor.

↓ TERRORHURTZ showing internal bulkhead structure.

Sir Killalot

The House Robots are built to have character, which often requires organic shapes and few of the flat or square edges that are typical of a lot of competition machines. That's why Sir Killalot is built on a tubular steel chassis, which was created in two main stages during its build.

Key components such as the drive modules and crushing claw were produced using computer-aided design (CAD), including Sir Killalot's base that holds its two tracked drive modules and batteries. This base was created as a simple tubular square that joined everything together and gave the team a solid platform on which to create the iconic machine you see today.

CAD designing can be very difficult and time-consuming to get right on a computer screen, as perception can prove very different to reality. Consequently the layout and dimensions for the main body and arms were determined by physically putting the pieces in position in the real world and seeing what suited Sir Killalot's character best. In this way measurements could be taken ready to manufacture the chassis. You'll notice that the new version of Sir Killalot is a lot more upright and aggressive in his stance than in the original series, to emphasise his dominance in the arena. You can see in the image on the left how the Robo Challenge team held the arms and body panels in different positions to visualize what worked best.

A tubular chassis design was used to give maximum flexibility in the design and build stages of Sir Killalot. Taking their dimensions from the manual positioning of parts allowed the team to cut their tubes to size and mount the shoulders and arms in place quickly and efficiently, providing the chassis with sufficient volume to contain the robot's internal components.

The tubular chassis also allowed huge flexibility in the positioning of major design elements, such as the head. This was placed in position so that tubes could be cut and tack-welded in place while still allowing it to be moved around slightly so that angles could be tweaked and heights adjusted to get the most out of the robot's character, before being welded solidly in place.

The internal chassis of Sir Killalot isn't very noticeable once the sculpted bodywork is mounted, which is why this style of chassis is perfect for a House Robot where visual characteristics are key.

⬇ **Modelling Sir Killalot's head and arms.**

⬅ **Sir Killalot's tubular chassis without body panels.**

Motors

The power of a robot is usually determined by the motors or engines that govern its drive and weapon systems. There's a vast range of motors to choose from, and, once again, each has its pros and cons.

Electric motors are the most common and often the simplest form of motor used in fighting robots. There are two key types of electric permanent magnet motor: the brushed and the brushless. Brushed motors are epitomized by your classic Scalextric type, where you add voltage across the two terminals to make the motor spin, which in turn spins the wheels. These types of motor are currently the most widely used in *Robot Wars*, due to their simplicity, low cost and general ruggedness.

In the original *Robot Wars* series, a favorite electric motor teams used was the Bosch 750. This was an extremely versatile 1hp motor that weighed in at just 9.3 pounds (4.2 kg). These motors were relatively cheap and, despite being just 24V, their industrial design meant they could be regularly over-volted by teams such as Tornado to get increased drive power.

Although it's still a popular motor (being used by Apollo in Series 8 and 9, for instance), many teams are moving away from it now because, as with most new technology, the price of high-end motors is steadily dropping, making them more affordable. These high-performance motors use rare earth magnets, which are typically two to three times stronger than the ferrite magnets used in the older industrial motors. This has huge benefits, as motors are now lighter and far more powerful.

Although brushed motors are very easy to control via a large range of off-the-shelf electronic speed controllers (ESCs), which can be bought to suit almost any motor voltage and current rating, their downside is that they use brushes rubbing on a commutator to transfer the voltage from the static wires to the rotating internals of the motor. Due to this rubbing the brushes wear down over time, which can lead to sparking and the generation of excessive heat, which permanently damages the motor.

Brushless motors get around this issue by spinning the magnets and not the internal windings, meaning there are no components rubbing together and causing friction or heat. However, brushless motors are a very recent addition to the *Robot Wars* arsenal and only a few teams have started to experiment with them. They're incredibly efficient, compact and use rare earth magnets. They also have much better power-to-weight ratios in comparison to brushed motors, leaving more weight and room available for other things, like weapons and armor.

↓ **ME0708 (10kW) and LEM 170-D127R (21kW) brushed DC motors.**

Andrew Marchant – Team Tornado

"We used the Bosch 750 due to its power, efficiency and cost. Wheelchair motors couldn't produce the torque we wanted, Iskra motors were heavy, comparatively expensive, inefficient, S2-rated and poorly cooled, while the Sinclair C5 motor was more expensive and harder to source – nailing down accurate specs on them was impossible too (despite a long phone conversation with the judge who had stock and was trying to flog them to us). The Briggs and Stratton lynch motor was just appearing on our radar at the time, but although awesome was too heavy for the 80 kg weight limit.

"We actually spent ages picking between the 24V and 12V versions of the Bosch motors, given Chaos 2 had successfully run the 12s at 24V before us. Of course, they aren't perfect motors for robots but I think the key thing is that they were cheap, and could easily be improved and adapted."

Ellis Ware - Pulsar/Magnetar

“ Are brushless motors worth it? In my mind, absolutely YES. When we nail this technology, it might well trigger the biggest evolution in robot combat designs ever. The space, weight, power and cost benefits are major, even next to the best brushed motors on the market. It's already a bit odd to design a new insect-class robot and not consider or use brushless, and I have no doubt that heavyweights will go the same way. Hopefully, a few years from now, robots like Pulsar and Big Nipper will be remembered as early adopters of the most obvious tech-shift since lithium batteries. ”

The reason why only a few teams are working with brushless motors is because of the added complexity involved in controlling them. Instead of two wires a brushless motor has three, which need to be powered in sequence by more complex electronics. This makes such motors more reliable, as they no longer have components that rub together, but their advanced ESCs need to be correctly configured to ensure they can start and accelerate the motor properly.

Though this isn't so difficult using off-the-shelf components if you only need to rotate the motor in one direction, such as for powering a spinning weapon, the drive systems in robots are under constant stress, accelerating the robot forwards, backwards and around, which presents a problem for the ESC on a brushless motor, which needs to know its exact position in order to know when to send the next pulse. It therefore ideally requires a sensored system from which the ESC can receive positional information from the motor that allows it to power each coil correctly. However, although in theory this sounds simple there are currently no off-the-shelf solutions, which is forcing teams to develop their own ESCs for *Robot Wars*.

Although a small, light and powerful motor sounds perfect, it brings with it certain issues. For instance, a smaller motor has a smaller thermal mass, which means it heats up much quicker under power. It's therefore very important to specify the right size of motor for your needs, and to make sure your brushless motor is much more powerful than what you actually need, since using over-powered motors means they'll be less stressed, will create less heat and ultimately be much more reliable in the arena.

Pulsar and Big Nipper have been two teams pushing the limits with brushless technology for both drive and weapons, showing the speed and power gains that can be achieved when used properly.

Internal combustion engines (ICE) can also be used in robots, and were extensively used in the original House Robots. They have their advantages in certain circumstances, as they're easy to control and very easy to get hold of cheaply by stripping them out of machines such as chainsaws and lawnmowers. Controlling such engines can be as simple as a servo opening and closing the throttle lever on the engine, negating the need for any complex electronics. Such engines are also designed to run for extended periods of time, from about half an hour to many hours continuously. With *Robot Wars* battles lasting only three minutes there isn't much risk of running out of fuel or battery power, which was always a problem for teams in the early series with the battery technology available.

Because of these factors, and being able to generate a lot of power, such engines were very well suited for spinning weapons. Matilda ran her chainsaw from a gas engine, Dead Metal's saw was powered by a gas strimmer engine, and even Sir Killalot used to have a large four-stroke engine to power the hydraulics for its weapons.

The biggest downside to internal combustion engines, though, is their reliability. If the robot gets flipped, or gets any air in its fuel lines, the engine would cut out. Most ICE robots couldn't restart their engines during a fight, and therefore the weapons just stopped working.

Another concern with gas engines is the risk of fire. The arena Flame Pit, coupled with Sergeant Bash's flamethrower, meant that having gas in your robot was a serious fire risk. Even Sir Killalot fell foul of the arena Flame Pit!

Although combustion engines can be very effective to power weaponry, they're not so simple to use for drive. To be competitive in the arena a robot needs to be capable of quick reactions from forward to reverse, but gas engines only turn in one direction. The complexity of gearboxes required to overcome this, or a hydraulic drive powered by the engine, are both heavy and costly in comparison to the simpler electric motors.

From Series 8 onwards the House Robots have been designed to use all-electric power where possible, and no longer use gas engines. With the improvement of electric motors and their increased size and weight, they're no less powerful than combustion motors, are more reliable, don't catch fire and require much less maintenance and refuelling. This provides Sir Killalot with a huge degree of flexibility, as his arm and claw movements are not only more powerful but can also be controlled either slowly and smoothly or fast and aggressively, which is far more complex with an engine.

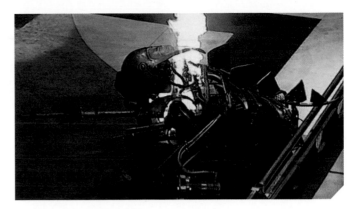

↑ **Sir Killalot catches fire.**

Power supply (batteries)

One of the biggest advancements in technology since the original *Robot Wars* left our screens has been batteries. In the original series the battery of choice was the sealed lead acid battery (SLA), with some teams stretching to more expensive nickel-cadmium (NiCd) batteries. SLA batteries were invented in 1859 by French physicist Gaston Planté. They were well developed, robust and reliable, and their ease of use and low cost meant they were the perfect choice for roboteers.

The biggest drawback of the SLA battery is its weight. Using high-end SLA batteries, teams would typically need approximately 25.1 pounds (11.4 kg) of batteries to get a 24V 15Ah (amp hours) set-up. This is a huge proportion of a robot's weight to dedicate to power storage, which led some teams to invest in a lighter, more costly technology, NiCd batteries. NiCds have approximately 50% higher gravimetric energy density than SLA batteries, meaning that for their weight they hold 50% more energy. This is of huge benefit to teams, because rather than needing 25.1 pounds (11.4kg) for batteries they now needed just 16.8 pounds (7.6 kg). (These weights are approximate and may vary, depending on manufacturer or model). This allowed teams to re-deploy the spare 8.3 pounds (3.8 kg) in other areas, such as weapons or armor. Even this is no match for the current breed of lithium batteries. NiCds contain toxic metals and are environmentally unfriendly, which has led to them being phased out and opened the gates to more modern technologies, such as lithium polymer (LiPo) batteries which have a much higher gravimetric energy density, meaning a pack of LiPo batteries of similar power to NiCds would weigh just 5.3 pounds (2.4 kg)! They maintain their voltage while discharging and are able to discharge faster, meaning your robot can draw more power for longer.

In addition to energy density, lithium polymer batteries are much more efficient when discharging at high rates. When you discharge a 15Ah SLA battery at very high currents, you would expect to only be able to use maybe 4Ah or 5Ah in total before the battery is flat, which is why robots often run low on power towards the end of a match. Lithium polymer batteries are much more efficient under high current draw, allowing the use of almost full capacity of the battery. So in addition to enjoying increased energy density you also don't need as much battery capacity to get through a fight.

Since, as we've seen, the House Robots don't play by the rules when it comes to

Grant Cooper – House Robot builder

❝ Always spec your lithium polymer batteries to leave at least 20% of their capacity remaining at the end of a battle, to keep them performing at their best. ❞

weight, energy density is irrelevant to them for the most part. In fact, Sir Killalot uses the additional weight of sealed lead acid batteries to his advantage. All eight of his high-power SLAs, totalling 36V and weighing 275 pounds (125 kg), are mounted at the very back of the chassis, to help balance out the weight of a competitor being gripped and lifted in the claw. Having so many large batteries means there's more than enough power to supply the high current draw from the motors and keep running for a full day of filming without a recharge.

Using SLAs also means that their batteries can be charged inside the House Robots, speeding up the preparation time before a battle.

← **Sir Killalot's rear battery compartment less than half full.**

Wiring

The wiring inside of a robot is one of the most overlooked elements of designing and building for *Robot Wars*, leading to a large number of failures and problems in the arena. It doesn't need to be complicated, but it's worth spending sufficient time on it at the design stage to work out what you need and ensure it'll fit and be accessible once the robot is completed.

Although every robot is wired differently and will have different power requirements, the following information will hopefully help you design a safe and reliable wiring loom.

↓ **PP3D needed its melted connectors cut off.**

Removable links

What is a removable link? Well, to start with it's the main safety feature required on every robot that enters the *Robot Wars* arena. It's a plug that goes directly in line with the batteries of the robot, which when taken out removes all power from the machine. Without this link in place it's impossible to drive the robot or activate its weapons accidentally.

Off-the-shelf power connectors are most commonly used for links so that they can be easily plugged in and removed without tools. However, the connectors need to be chosen carefully to ensure that they're rated above the maximum current draw of your entire machine when in use. If your link isn't capable of taking the current it can melt or fuse together, making it very difficult to remove.

Most robots generally require a single link for the entire robot. However, there are occasions where two or more links are needed. For instance, if the drive system is running at a different voltage to the weapon system (*eg* the drive motors running at 24V and weapon system at 28V) then two independent links would be required, one drive link and one weapon link. It's also advisable to have an independent link for any high-power or high-speed electric weapons even if they use the same battery pack as the drive.

If the robot can drive upside down (even if it has a self-righter) then the links need to be accessible when inverted as well as upright. This usually requires another link or set of links underneath the robot.

The connectors can be very large, so accommodating up to four of them in accessible positions after the design stage can be very difficult.

Electrical connections

Electrical connections in a robot need to be kept to an absolute minimum where possible, as they're a common point of failure in the machine. The most common failure points in wiring joints or connectors are:

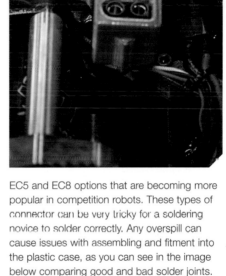

- Fatigue of solder on joints. Always make sure your joints are well soldered and heat-shrunk to avoid failure from fatigue. Making sure the joint isn't under any stress (eg stretched cables) or on a bend will help to minimize the effects of fatigue.
- Melted connectors. Another source of failure is overheating and melting. Teams try and save weight anywhere they can, and using smaller connectors can help dramatically; however, you must always make sure your connectors are rated high enough for the current your components are pulling.
- Disconnected connectors. With all the bashing and impacts a robot takes in the arena, the most common failure in wiring is the connectors simply becoming unplugged! Hard-mounted connectors (bolted to the chassis) are more susceptible to these shocks, so it's advisable to physically hold each side together. This can be achieved using heat shrink over connectors that aren't frequently disconnected, or a cable tie/tape for connectors that are used more frequently.

Various connectors can be chosen depending on your particular electronics skill level. For anyone who struggles with soldering, there are options for crimping. Anderson connectors are very robust and solid and can be either soldered or crimped using a cheap hydraulic crimping tool.

If you're competent at soldering, you might want to consider the much smaller and lighter

EC5 and EC8 options that are becoming more popular in competition robots. These types of connector can be very tricky for a soldering novice to solder correctly. Any overspill can cause issues with assembling and fitment into the plastic case, as you can see in the image below comparing good and bad solder joints.

Almost overflowing!

↑ **Sir Killalot's blue power LEDs shine through his back.**

During the safety checks at *Robot Wars* all wiring is inspected to make sure there are no bare or damaged wires. This includes wires rubbing on sharp edges or trapped between components and any other issues that could lead to the wires shorting on the chassis or other components. To avoid this, all connections must be properly covered in heat shrink or proper electric tape.

Another key part of the safety check is to ensure that each robot has a power light, which is an LED in line with the main battery source. When this LED light is on the robot is active and dangerous. The LED must turn off when the link is removed, and not be powered through a separate receiver battery pack.

These rules also apply to the House Robots. Sir Killalot has blue LEDs in his back to indicate power is on, and has two independent links, one for the drive power and one for the hydraulic weapons. Although the weapons and drive are all powered off the same 36V batteries the links are independent, so that he can be safely driven without any risk of the weapons becoming active, and vice versa. This is very useful when testing and making repairs, as we know exactly which parts of the robot are active.

Control systems

When people think of robots, they often think of complex and expensive control systems that take massive amounts of programming and require enormous skill to learn. In *Robot Wars*, however, that doesn't need to be the case, most teams' control systems being tried and tested off-the-shelf components that anyone can use.

The rules state that all robots must use 2.4ghz spread spectrum technology for their radio-controlled wireless systems (transmitter and receiver). It sounds complicated, but it uses the same radio controllers that are sold in model shops for RC cars and planes, starting at a very affordable level for a very basic system up to thousands of pounds for a really high-end radio that has more functions than you'd ever need in a robot.

As with most things, you tend to get what you pay for, and we'd always recommend avoiding the temptation of a cheap bargain and investing in a good-quality transmitter and receiver set. With something as dangerous as a robot it's worth spending that little bit extra on the one piece of vital equipment that directly controls everything your robot does!

Choosing a transmitter can be daunting when you don't know what to look for, but

← Two excellent-
quality radio
transmitters with
six channels and
fully programmable
functions.

a safe bet for most robots would be a good quality six-channel set.

The number of channels on a radio transmitter relates to the number of things you want to move or control on your robot. For example, to drive a normal two-wheeled robot you'd need one channel for forwards and backwards for each motor. That's two channels used just for drive. Then weapon systems will usually require at least one channel to work the valves or motor.

Although in the above example we've only used three channels, the extra flexibility of having six would allow you to choose if you want the weapon activated by a joystick, a switch or even a button. Using a switch or a button allows you to wire-in an extended switch so that another team member can activate the weapons without the additional cost of a second radio set (although this may void your warranty!).

The transmitter sends the driver's inputs through the air to the receiver, which usually comes with the radio transmitter. The receiver holds the information in the failsafe positions that you set so that the robot won't move or operate if the radio's battery runs or if signal is lost. This failsafe is required on every channel, and set in the receiver when the transmitter and receiver are bound together. This process varies between models but is always clearly explained in the user manual.

To actually control the electric motors in a robot we need an electronic speed controller (ESC). This reads the information from the receiver and controls the motors accordingly, allowing for smooth and controlled driving. ESCs are mostly off-the-shelf products, and for brushed motors are available in a huge variety to suit almost any power requirements.

The features of ESCs can also vary greatly, and choosing the right one depends on your needs. To start with, do you need dual or single channel? Dual channel ESCs are perfect for the drive of most robots. Using two

↓ Switch wires can be extended easily.

↑ **RageBridge 2 designed by Charles Guan, roboteer.**

→ **Sabertooth 2x60A.**

→ **Vex BB 300A 50V controller, single channel.**

motors for the drive, dual ESCs will control both sides independently in one smaller package, which saves on wiring too. Single channel ESCs are ideal for weapons where a single motor is being used. They can also offer greater flexibility for mounting, as they tend to be smaller.

Mixing

To make a robot drive forwards we ideally want to push the joystick forwards, but without mixing this will control just one side of the robot, making it spin in circles. A mixer will control both sides of the robot, allowing forward/backward and left/right joysticks movements to move the robot where you want with ease. Dual channel ESCs usually have mixing built into them that you can turn on or off, which saves a lot of hassle playing with the settings in your transmitter to set it. However, if you prefer single-channel ESCs you'll find that most reasonable quality transmitters also have channel mixing built in. In most circumstances, as long as one or the other is active then your robot will drive in the direction you want with a single joystick.

Battery eliminator circuit

A lot of ESCs will have something called a battery eliminator circuit (BEC) built in. This is an internal circuit that regulates your robot's main battery voltage going into the ESC into a low-power 5V supply, to power your receiver and other circuitry. This is really useful to have in an ESC, so it's something you need to consider when purchasing. If the ESC you're thinking of buying doesn't have one you can purchase individual BECs to wire in line with the rest of your robot. A BEC can be sourced relatively cheaply from radio-control equipment suppliers.

Power and voltage

The biggest factor when choosing the correct ESC is to make sure that it's specified for your power needs. Make sure both the voltage and the current draw of your motors are well within the limits of your ESC to ensure maximum reliability.

The drive motors in Sir Killalot are seriously powerful and capable of pulling a truck, so need some equally powerful ESCs to suit. His 4QD 300As are used at 36V on each motor with current limiting in place, which allows him to use huge amounts of power when needed, yet doesn't allow that current draw to get too high and damage either the motors or the ESC. This means everything stays cool and very reliable. This is a total of 29hp just on the drive.

Gyros

An electronic gyro is a small electronic unit used in model planes and helicopters to keep them heading in a set direction. If they take a knock or the wind blows them around, the gyro corrects their position and carries on in a straight line.

Gyros, which sit between the receiver and the ESC, have become increasingly popular in robots over the years, particularly in faster robots like Thor and TERRORHURTZ that are normally difficult to drive. The only issue with running a gyro is that the mixing needs to be

after the gyro, so either the ESC needs the mixer built in or a separate mixer needs to be added between the gyro and the ESC.

↑ **4QD 300A single channel as used in the House Robots.**

Drive systems

The obvious choice for most teams' drive systems is to use wheels. They're cheap, reliable and can give plenty of grip. Two-wheel drive can be as simple as bolting a wheel direct to the end of a gearbox shaft and you're good to go!

For added grip and stability, four-wheel drive or even six-wheel drive – as used by Behemoth and Storm 2 – can easily be implemented by chains or belts to improve the performance of your robot.

Choosing how many wheels your robot needs largely depends on your weapon. Most flippers, axes and spinners tend to lean more towards a two-wheel-drive set-up, both to save weight for additional armor and to increase the agility of the robot. These types of robot rely heavily on their weapons, with the drive system being used more to aim the weapon in the right direction, where grip and power aren't of as much concern.

↙ **NPC T64 motor gearbox and wheel assembly ready to bolt into a robot.**

↓ **Storm 2 utilizing six wheels for maximum grip and performance.**

Robots that really rely on their pushing ability, such as Tornado and Storm 2, tend to use more wheels. The extra wheels give them more grip and make driving the robot more accurate and predictable, the extra grip allowing to put more power into the floor and use the robot itself as a weapon.

However, wheels aren't the only option on *Robot Wars*, and other drive systems have been used to great effect over the years.

Tracks

Tank-style tracks are still used occasionally by competitors due to their huge advantage in grip over standard wheels. Other than looking excellent, they also have additional benefits. Steering with tracks is very precise and makes a robot very predictable and easy to control due to the extra grip and power required to make the robot steer. As Track-Tion showed in Series 10, flippers and pushers find it extremely difficult to get under them from the side to push or flip them over.

The downside to tracks is mainly their weight and vulnerability to spinners. The additional power required to turn also means more powerful motors are required, and that can mean larger ESCs and batteries, all adding to weight and cost. For these reasons very few teams choose this method of drive nowadays. Not so the House Robots, tracks being the drive system of choice for mighty Sir Killalot. Other than the aesthetics of tracks, which look very industrial, Sir Killalot's provide him with a really solid base that can apply full power to the arena floor without the danger of wheel-spinning. His incredible grip means that nothing can push him around, and flippers can't get under his sides to flip him. With almost 30hp in drive power he can turn with ease and at great speed to out-maneuver even the best of competition machines.

Walkers and shufflers

Walkers and shufflers are rare on *Robot Wars*, but have been used to great effect over the years.

Walkers, which must have 2° of freedom on each leg, are eligible for an overall weight increase of 77 pounds (35 kg) for heavyweights and 9 pounds (4 kg) for featherweights. Walkers are complex and heavy drive systems, which can often be delicate and easy to damage. Although it's rare to see a walking fighting robot, the extra weight advantage could make this drive system worthwhile. Sadly, one of the only walker bots in *Robot Wars* history, Eleven, lost its first and only fight.

Shufflers, on the other hand, have proven very successful. A shuffler is a walking system made of legs that rotate with a gear or cam system in only one plane (forwards and backwards). A shuffler gets an additional weight bonus of 33 pounds (15 kg) for heavyweights and 3.3 pounds (1.5 kg) for featherweights, which can give them a big advantage.

↓ **Track-Tion used tank-style tracks during Series 10.**

→ **Walking robots, yes please!**

One of the most competitive shufflers in *Robot Wars* was Drillzilla. Drillzilla was the first of its kind, making use of the current rule set at the time that allowed for double the usual weight limit. Back then there was no distinction between shuffler robots and walking robots, and teams agreed that the bending of the rules was not within the best interests of the sport, so an amendment was made to separate shuffler cam systems and walkers into separate categories. Drillzilla nevertheless proved that speed and power could be achieved with this system, and with the extra 33-pound (15 kg) weight incentive they offer in the current series they're certainly worth looking into.

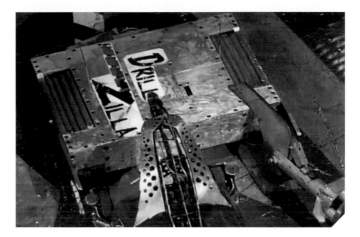

Pneumatic systems

↑ **Drillzilla gets crushed by Razer and Sir Killalot.**

Pneumatic weapons are widely used in *Robot Wars*. Using compressed CO_2 (carbon dioxide) stored as liquid in tanks on board the robot at 750psi, such weapons can be incredibly fast and powerful. Weapons such as flippers, axes, spikes and grabbers can all be powered effectively through the use of CO_2.

Two main types of pneumatic system are used in robots: full pressure and low pressure. The basics of a full-pressure system comprise the main CO_2 bottle, a buffer tank or reservoir and then a valve leading into the pneumatic cylinder

to activate the weapon. This is a nice and very simple set-up that's been used by the majority of flippers in the UK since the early years of *Robot Wars*, and is very cost-effective. High-pressure systems have real benefits in terms of raw power. For the same-sized pneumatic cylinder, the force applied is far greater than that of a low-pressure system. The downside of this system, however, is that it inherently uses more CO_2, meaning either less use of the weapon or the need for more CO_2 to be stored in the robot.

Low-pressure systems are very similar to

↓ **Full pressure CO_2 gives Apollo all the power it needs to take on Shunt!**

↑ **Behemoth showing low-pressure pneumatics work well in the arena.**

high-pressure, except that they have a pressure regulator directly between the main CO_2 bottle and the buffer tank. The regulator reduces the pressure coming out of the CO_2 tanks to around 0–200psi in general. Robots such as Thor, TERRORHURTZ and Behemoth run low-pressure systems between 110–200psi that perform brilliantly. These robots tend to get a lot more use out of their weapons in a battle than others, even when using the CO_2 to return their weapons once fired.

Pneumatics aren't just used in fighting robots, but are in widespread industrial use worldwide. High-speed robotic production lines have made use of pneumatic systems for many years, offering a highly efficient system that requires minimal maintenance or human intervention. Although *Robot Wars* machines run on higher pressures, the principles of compressed air moving pneumatic cylinders via a series of valves is very much the same.

Safety requirements for pneumatic robots

Safety is critical when making use of potentially high-powered pneumatic systems. Consequently *Robot Wars* have a strict set of rules to ensure that the use of CO_2 is made as safe as possible, and robots' pneumatic systems are carefully scrutinized during the safety checks at every event:

- Main CO_2 bottles must be off the shelf (usually fire extinguishers) and be in good condition, with no dents, cuts or other issues. The bottle must have a burst disc fitted (standard on CO_2 bottles) that's rated to blow if the pressure rises too high.
- Pressure relief valves are required in all pneumatic robots. A pressure relief valve ensures that the CO_2 in the system is vented to the atmosphere if the pressure exceeds the system's rated pressure.
- Dump valves are again a requirement on all pneumatic robots. These allow the pressure in the entire system to be dumped into the atmosphere quickly to make the robot safe to handle.
- Weapon locking bars must also be used at all times when the robot isn't in use. A locking bar is a device that can easily slide through the chassis and weapon to lock it in position. This allows the robot to be armed-up without the risk of the weapon activating.

Hydraulic systems

→ **That's not what hydraulic oil should be doing…**

Hydraulic weapons have made a big impact on *Robot Wars*, especially with Razer. The UK and double world champions were about the first team to really show how competitive a hydraulic machine can be.

Hydraulics work in a similar way to pneumatics, but instead of storing compressed air in a tank to move the pistons, fluid is pumped at high pressure. This is a lot slower than pneumatics but typically runs at far higher pressures (up to a maximum of 10,000psi in the rules).

Unlike the air in pneumatics, the fluid in a hydraulic system isn't vented or dumped into the atmosphere. By recirculating the fluid, hydraulics don't have an issue with how many times the weapon can be activated, as long as the batteries in the robot are capable of supplying the power required.

Because of the lower speed and higher force of hydraulic weapons they tend to be best suited to crushing and grabbing, when precision rather than brute force is key. Kan-Opener was an excellent example of how hydraulics could be utilized in a fighting robot.

With their increased availability and improvements in their motor technology, hydraulic systems are now capable of producing far more power than Razer had. Tiberius, a robot based on the concept of Razer, has been improved greatly since winning the University Challenge in *Robot Wars Extreme Series 2*. It originally had 3.3 tons (3 t) of crushing power at its tip, though after years of improvement and with modern motors Tiberius now has around 6.6 tons (6 t) of crushing force.

The types of weaponry in which hydraulics can be successfully utilized are limited, and due to the higher pressures involved each component tends to be much heavier than its pneumatic counterpart. Add to this the complexity of needing to bleed every last bit of air out of the system and you can understand why, despite their impressive power, hydraulic

↑ Kan-Opener's sharpened its claws ready to crush.

machines are still few and far between.

Due to their common use in industrial and agricultural equipment, however, hydraulics are readily available off the shelf. From Jaws of Life rescue equipment to JCBs, hydraulics are used as reliable workhorses wherever high-powered equipment is needed. Which makes them perfect for mighty Sir Killalot. With robust and proven off-the-shelf products, Sir Killalot's hydraulic systems can be repaired quickly and efficiently when needed, and don't need refilling before each battle. The extra force they provide enable him to lift three times his competitors' maximum weight on each arm, and crush with over 2.2 tons (2 t) of force at the tip of his claw, all with smoothness and precision.

← Sir Killalot's elbow is one huge hydraulic cylinder producing 12 tons (11 t) of force!

Bodywork and armor

→ Coyote showing off its steampunk theme.

↓ TERRORHURTZ being repaired with armor removed.

↓↓ Apollo's small access holes can make it tricky to repair in a rush.

The outer armor and bodywork of a robot can really define its character, so it's an important part of its design. When designing your armor there are a number of key things to consider:

Style

Normally, by this stage you'll have a reasonable idea of what you want your robot to look like. Is it a polished sleek modern design, or an industrial steampunk machine that can make use of pipes and fittings? These aesthetic choices will help guide how you make your armor throughout the design stage. The theme or character can be portrayed through paint, decoration or even just by polishing the artwork of your finished product.

Accessibility

A commonly overlooked issue is the accessibility or serviceability of your robot before and after a battle. When competing at *Robot Wars* you can often have as little as two hours to strip down your machine and make repairs, which means its body armor needs to be removable or everything inside has to be very accessible!

This can often cause problems with a monocoque chassis, where the armor is an integral part of the chassis and isn't removable. Robots such as Apollo have multiple removable panels on top to help get components in and out of the chassis. Other robots such as TERRORHURTZ can remove the entire outer armor by taking out just a few bolts to allow easy access to every internal component.

Materials

Material choice is always difficult. Cost, weight and available tools will all have a large impact on the materials you opt for.

One of the most widely used metals for robot armor is Hardox, a wear steel (*ie* abrasion-resistant) used mostly on agricultural equipment, JCBs and military vehicles. Readily available all around the UK, it has excellent properties that make it ideal for robots. However, though like most steels it can be easily welded, cutting and drilling Hardox is significantly harder than mild steel, so designs must be carefully thought out before you start work. It's also very heavy, so it

can be difficult to armor an entire robot in the same thickness of metal. Some teams therefore use Hardox on the front but lighter armor around the rest of the machine.

Titanium is another common choice for roboteers, and can often be found cheap online or at scrapyards. Working with titanium can be difficult, but the weight-savings gained can be well worthwhile. Teams such as Big Nipper use titanium almost exclusively for armor, mounted on top of an all-aluminium lightweight chassis.

Armour doesn't need to be made from metal, though. Gabriel is a prime example of how plastic robots can stand up to some of the toughest machines in the competition. HDPE (high-density polyethylene) is a very affordable plastic that can be bought in sheets or blocks, and is very easy to cut and drill with basic hand tools. The really good thing about HDPE is that it's really flexible which means it acts like a shock absorber between a robot's body and the important components inside. This flexibility was clearly demonstrated by Gabriel surviving an entire battle despite taking hit after hit from Carbide directly to its wheels.

With spinning weapons becoming so powerful, the thickness and hardness of your armor won't stop their massive shocks from being transmitted throughout a robot's entire internal system. By looking at the way HDPE performs in these circumstances, teams are now beginning to rubber-mount more solid armor, like Hardox, to their chassis. This provides excellent protection from spinning weapons, whilst at the same time dampening the impacts so that they don't damage internal components.

As well as rubber-mounting and material thickness, armor can often be improved dramatically by angling it sharply down towards the floor so that spinners just glance off, while removing all sharp edges and corners means weapons can't grip on to an edge. TERRORHURTZ used these principles to ensure it could take on and beat Carbide in its head-to-head battle.

↖ **TERRORHURTZ showing its strong front armor and vulnerable sides.**

↑ **Gabriel doesn't give up.**

← **TERRORHURTZ shows Carbide who's boss.**

Craig Collias – Gabriel

❝ HDPE is a material we've been using for many years now, but it has to be used in the correct way or it will fail. It works best when it's anchored to the robot in such a way that it's free to flex as much as possible. It's this distortion that soaks up the force of impacts. For example, on Gabriel the wheels are doing several jobs. Firstly they're wheels, obviously; secondly they're the side armor for the robot; and lastly they're used to drain the energy from spinners like Carbide by flexing, and under extreme load tearing it puts sufficient strain on the opponent's weapon and drive that it can cause failure. Used correctly, weight for weight HDPE can be more durable than the hardest steel. ❞

The weapons are what *Robot Wars* is all about. Without some form of weaponry that can cause problems for your opponent, your robot is an undersized, remote-controlled trolley. When it comes to weapons the great thing about *Robot Wars* is that there's no best weapon, no single solution that means you'll win.

The multitude of possibilities and solutions means *Robot Wars* is an extremely creative environment where, quite often, something new and quirky can take on the established teams and cause a major upset. In Series 9 the mighty Carbide used its destructive bar-spinner to take the trophy without sustaining even a scratch. Not a single opponent lasted the full three minutes of combat. So when Carbide returned for Series 10 having made even more improvements to their formidable machine, everyone in the pits was running scared, hoping not to be drawn against the reigning champions. It seemed like a big spinner weapon was the way to win.

These are the truly ingenious robots that turn the whole *Robot Wars* concept upside down. They highlighted another way to win, emphatically underlining the fact that there *isn't* a best weapon or design. In the entire history of *Robot Wars*, axe-armed robots are the only type that haven't won the main series. However, robots such as the relentless TERRORHURTZ prove that this doesn't mean

axes are uncompetitive, because no two weapon designs are the same. So let's take a look at the various weapon classifications into which most designs fall, looking not only at the strengths of each weapon type but also their vulnerabilities.

Flippers and lifter weapons

Weapons designed to lift and turn over their opponent can be extremely effective in battle. They're tactically used to get other robots on to their backs, where they're vulnerable to being pushed into the arena's hazards and the House Robots.

Lifters tend to be slower moving and more controlled devices than flippers, being powered by electric motors or low-pressure/low-flow pneumatic systems. This gives you the option of using your weapon tactically. A lifter weapon was most famously used by Panic Attack, which won *Robot Wars* Series 2. Panic Attack were able to use their electric lifting forks to slowly and precisely lift their opponents just enough so take their wheels off the floor. All they had to do then was accurately maneuver their opponents over the Pit and drop them in. This is a tactic that requires a smooth driver and accurate weapons operator but is very rewarding when used correctly.

By contrast, flippers are high impact, instant

⇩ **Carbide tries to take on the House Robots after being crowned Series 9 champions. Killalot and Shunt deal with him rather abruptly!**

fire weapons. Most commonly powered by full-pressure CO_2 (ie CO_2 without a regulator to lower the pressure), flippers force their high-pressure gas directly into pneumatic cylinders to get an instant *bang*! Rather than relying on the accuracy and control of a lifter, the flipper is designed to launch its opponents into the air with the intention of launching them into the OPZs, the other hazards or the best strategy – straight out of the arena altogether! Chaos 2 was the first robot to deploy a flipper with great success, winning both Series 3 and Series 4 of *Robot Wars*.

So as can be seen, the lifter and flipper are both extremely effective weapons, but they rely on a very low ground clearance in order to get their weapon underneath opponents' robots. The major disadvantage of both, however, is that they only have a limited amount of high-pressure gas available, which means they have to use their weapon wisely and economically to ensure they don't run out of gas midway through a battle, which would render it redundant. They also pack such a kick that it's imperative to correctly time the flips to avoid flipping themselves over on their backs.

Battling against a robot of this type is extremely frustrating, and it's difficult to keep your nerve when your machine is upside down and trying to self-right to get back into the battle!

Crushers and grippers

Crushers and grippers can be extremely effective and versatile weapons. They don't use inertia to cause damage like most robots do. Instead they use brute force to crush, puncture and twist their opponents into submission.

Crushers tend to be slow weapons powered by electric actuators or high-pressure hydraulic systems similar to digger arms. They require very good timing, low ground clearance and good drivers to use effectively. However, they're also the only weapon type that gives you complete control of a battle. Once your opponent is locked in your jaws, there literally is nothing they can do; they're at your mercy and must wait to be released before they can get back into the fight. Being in your grip not only unsettles them but it actually gives you time to stop, take a second and decide on your next strategy.

↑ **Robo Savage launches Dee into the air with a big flip.**

↓ **Flipper-equipped Apollo – wearing a few battle scars here – was the Series 8 champion.**

Another big advantage of the crusher, in particular those that crush vertically, is that it specifically targets the top surface of its opponent. Due to the increasing power of spinning weapons over the years, teams tend to put most of their armor on the sides of their robots, the areas where spinners make contact. Which leaves them with vulnerable top surfaces that a crusher can exploit.

Crushers like nice boxy types of opponent, with flat top surfaces that they can grab. This is because robots with steep sides, such as Dominator 2 and TERRORHURTZ, are extremely difficult for a crusher to actually get hold of, which renders it almost redundant.

Naturally there are downsides to all weapons, and the crusher certainly has its critics. Firstly, being a relatively slow-moving weapon your maneuvering has to be very precise in order to catch fast robots. So if you want to be at all competitive a crusher robot certainly need two operators, one to drive the robot and the other solely concentrating on timing the weapon to perfection.

Another thing to consider is the raw power required to actually cause damage to the opponent. Tiberius, one of the most powerful crushers around, still struggles to puncture some of the modern armors in today's *Robot Wars*, despite having 6.6 tons (6 t) of force on the tip of its beak! All this force has to go somewhere, though, so it's imperative a crusher robot's weapon and chassis are able to cope with the force running through it.

This makes the crusher robot one of the most technically challenging to build, especially if it has some serious crushing power. When they're built right, though, they can be an incredible force in the arena. One of the most famous robots of all time used a hydraulic crusher so successfully they won *Robot Wars* Series 5, two world championships, the Southern Annihilator, an International League championship and two All Stars championships, along with multiple Best Design awards. I am, of course, talking about the legendary Razer.

One of the most successful fighting robots of all time, Razer was so accurately driven by Ian Lewis and Simon Scott that, Ian tells me, they could target a weak point on the opponent the size of a coin and get it every time. This high level of driving accuracy was, of course, critical to Razer winning so many trophies. Even when they were up against a robot with armor they couldn't penetrate they could still grapple and wrestle their opponents down the Pit or into the CPZs.

Axes and flails

Axes have been proven over the years to be powerful weapons designed to puncture, bludgeon and rattle their opponents into submission. They're normally powered by low-pressure CO_2 (ie regulated down to between 10–16 bar) or high-power electric motors, and conveniently also work as self-righting mechanisms.

⬇ **Razer grapples with Kill-E-Crank-E.**

⬇⬇ **Andron 4000's crushing jaw pierces the belly of Concussion.**

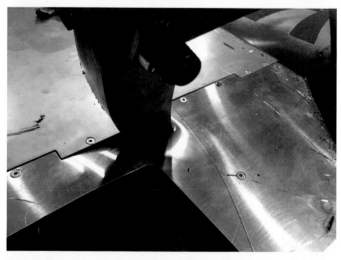

Self-righting

One critical area of a fighting robot is its ability to self-right during a battle. Despite a great start, Razer was famously knocked out of Series 2 by being tipped on its side and having no way to get itself upright. Today flipper weapons are so powerful that even the best teams can't risk entering the arena without some way of recovering from a flip. After all, it only takes one shot for a flipper to get a robot on its back, so the likelihood of it happening is very high!

So, what's the best method for a robot to self-right? That depends entirely on the design of your machine. There are a number of ways to tackle the problem. The most obvious one, which is used by almost every flipper and axe robot, is to use the weapon itself to self-right. Robots like Thor and Rapid have specifically designed their armor so that when the robot is upside down, it lands perfectly on its weapon, which can be fired immediately to get them back on its wheels. Some flipper and axe robots even have a special "self-righting" weapon mode, which reduces the power to their weapon just enough to roll the robot back over without being so much that the robot is launched high in the air, wasting precious gas.

The second method is to create a dedicated SRIMECH, or self-righting mechanism. Robots such as Hypnodisc and Magnetar, for instance, deploy specific levers and arms to lift the robot back on to its wheels. Such mechanisms inevitably add extra complexity and weight to a robot, but if you have a weapon that can't double as a self-righter it may be your only choice.

Finally there are those that can't use their weapon to self-right and yet don't want to waste weight on a separate SRIMECH. Rather than bothering to self-right at all, robots such as Carbide and Sabretooth design their robots cleverly so that they can run both ways up! Invertible robots, as they're called, can drive just as well upside down as the right way up. This is naturally the fastest way to continue battling when you've been flipped over, as you don't have to waste time self-righting. It does restrict the design of your robot, though, since the wheels have to be clear on both top and bottom, which means you have to design a low, flat shape. Also, when your robot is upside down the controls are backwards – forwards becomes

backwards and vice versa – so it takes a great driver to be able to switch how they drive when their robot is inverted. After all, if you lose your sense of direction it would be very easy for your opponent to take advantage and you might even inadvertently drive into a hazard!

← Thor uses its axe to self-right.

↓ Carbide battles on against TERRORHURTZ despite being upside down!

↓↓ Magnetar test their self-righting arm in the pits.

John Reid – TERRORHURTZ

" While axe weapons are difficult to aim accurately, they have a number of advantages. They attack from the top, where robots are less likely to be heavily armored. And because the weapon is overhead, it allows you to have seamless front armor. They also constitute a built-in and very effective self-righting mechanism, providing a significant weight-saving. "

↑ **Thor lays down the hammer blows on Shockwave.**

The interesting thing with axes and hammers is that they're rarely designed to actually puncture their opponents. This would cause the two robots to be locked together, making your weapon redundant until it can be freed. Instead they opt for the "blunt force trauma" approach, using high-energy impacts to send shocks into the opponent's robot causing its internal components to fail or crumple. A downside to pneumatic axes, however, is that – just like flippers – even though they're regulated to lower pressures the number of blows they can make is limited during a battle, so it's vital to ensure that each strike is accurate in order not to waste gas. Like a vertical crusher robot, axes exploit the weaker top armor of their opponents. They can fire in less than a quarter of a second, an explosive speed that requires

→ **Nick preps the tenacious TERRORHURTZ for battle.**

split second reactions from the operator to ensure that every blow strikes home.

The key to building a good axe robot is getting the balance right between accelerating the axe fast enough that it causes damage but not so fast that it makes the entire robot jump and become unstable. This instability makes it arguably one of the more difficult robots to make competitive. However, they're incredibly tenacious if they can pin an opponent up against the arena wall and get in multiple hits.

Although an axe robot has never won the TV series of *Robot Wars*, the iconic machine TERRORHURTZ constructed by legendary builder John Reid proves that axes can be extremely competitive. TERRORHURTZ has made it to several finals in the past and was the first robot to comprehensively beat

Carbide. It regularly makes teams panic in the pits when they know they have to face it. The majority of well-known teams always make special armor panels for their upper surfaces of their robots in case they have to take on TERRORHURTZ's mighty axe. Not many robots are so revered. Everyone knows that, on a good day, there are not many machines that can survive a relentless hammering from TERRORHURTZ.

Spinning weapons

There are two types of spinning weapon: saw blades, such as are used to great effect by the House Robot Dead Metal; and flywheels, which are designed to impact rather than cut.

Let's take a look at the saws first, which are rarely seen in *Robot Wars* because robots don't tend to be easy objects to cut. Not only are saws and grinders very easily damaged by even the lightest of bumps, but also – though angle grinders and saws are designed to cut through literally anything – their biggest problem in *Robot Wars* is that the object you want to cut through is usually trying to run away! It's therefore extremely difficult to utilize a saw weapon effectively unless you have some way of keeping your opponent still. However, that's exactly what Dead Metal does, using his huge pincers to grab hold of other robots so that he can spin up his saw and chop into them. His saw literally slices through even the toughest of armor, being designed not to cut,

but to melt its way through – which is why you see a great shower of sparks whenever he has a robot in his grips.

The second type of spinner weapon is traditionally called a flywheel. These come in all sorts of shapes and sizes, from Hypnodisc-like discs to Sabretooth-style drum spinners. The principle of these weapons is the opposite of saws. A saw has lots of teeth or abrasive edges that are designed to cut away tiny segments as each tooth passes through. The saw is also driven by the power and torque of the motor, which means it needs a particular amount of force pushing the saw into its opponent to work. Too little force and no cutting is achieved, too much force and the blade comes to a grinding halt.

A flywheel-type spinner is the polar opposite. Instead of cutting, the aim is to spin as much mass as fast as possible to give the weapon as much kinetic energy as can be achieved. Once up to speed, the idea is to transfer that kinetic energy into the opponent in one big impact. The flywheels don't have lots of saw-like teeth – instead they use as few as possible, which are much larger and chunkier. Most teams' flywheels have just two teeth, while some teams engineer balanced discs with just a single tooth which is optimum for what we call "engagement." Good engagement is critical when it comes to spinners. Engagement is how much of the spinner tooth bites into the opponent on impact. This is critical if you want

← **Dead Metal's blade melts through its victim.**

→ Carbide's array of interchangeable spinning bars.

↓ Aftershock also has interchangeable weaponry but these are different weights depending on how much armor they add for different opponents. Their favorite is the heaviest vertical disc.

to make the biggest impacts possible, which is where the different spinner styles come in.

It's easy to calculate how much potential engagement your spinner may have when you're in the design stages. Take a spinning disc with four large teeth on the outer rim, let's say it has a 1 meter circumference, meaning there will be approximately 250 millimeters between each tooth, depending on the design. Imagine this disc is spinning at 1,200 revolutions per minute (rpm), divide that by 60 seconds and that's 20 revolutions per second. As the disc has a 1 meter circumference that means it's moving at 20 meters per second. Each full rotation takes just 0.05 of a second. As the disc has four teeth, the time it takes for each tooth to pass is just 0.0125 of a second! So that's the tiny bit

of time you have to get a bit of your opponent between the spinner teeth.

In this example our robot drives at 2 meters per second. If the opponent is stationary that means after 0.0125 seconds (the time between each tooth impacting) the robot will have travelled 25 millimeters. That's the maximum engagement when hitting a stationary object with the disc at full speed and the robot driving at 2 meters per second towards the target. Naturally the engagement increases when the opponent is driving towards you and decreases if it's moving away. 25 millimeters of engagement isn't too bad but in reality it's still unlikely, as you would have to engage with the opponent at the perfect moment, just after one tooth passes, to ensure the maximum time for your next tooth to come around.

With all spinners, the aim is to increase the potential engagement as much as possible, as this will impart more energy from your weapon into the opponent. Too little engagement and the spinner grinds instead of impacting. One way to increase the engagement on this example is to reduce the number of teeth on the disc. Let's use the exact same setup with one change: reduce the number of teeth from four to two. Halving the number of teeth means there's twice as much space between them, meaning there'll be twice as much time from one tooth passing to the next one passing – 0.025 of a second now. This will double our potential engagement to 50 millimeters, which

↑ **Sabretooth sports a slender but heavy spinning drum.**

will create a much bigger impact! This is one element that teams put a lot of thought into when designing a spinning weapon.

As with all *Robot Wars* machines there is no best solution; every design type has its advantages and its compromises. Drum-style spinners allow for a wide and compact spinning section, which is great for keeping the machine compact. It also gives you a very wide attack point, meaning you don't need armor at the front of your robot. It's also easier to make an invertible machine – a robot that can run upside down – with a drum. However, the limitation with drums is that because they're so compact and have a relatively small diameter, you have to spin them faster to get a good tooth speed. You're also limited in the size of the teeth, which reduces your potential engagement further.

A spinning disc like Hypnodisc and PP3D means you get larger diameter discs, which could give you a very nice flywheel design. This is when the majority of the weight of the spinning disc is around the outside edge, meaning you're using the weight of the disc more economically to give your weapon as much energy as possible. You're also not limited in the size of your teeth, meaning the spinner engagement can be very good. The disadvantage with a disc is that because of the larger diameter you may need a larger chassis to house it. Having so much mass around the edge of the disc, although better for storing energy, also requires more power from the motor to spin it up.

Bar spinners such as Carbide try to take engagement to the extreme. By compromising on the flywheel effect of having the mass on the outside of the spinner, having a rotating bar means you literally have no limits on the amount of engagement. This trade-off increases wind resistance of spinning bars, which in turn increases current draw for your motor and places more stress on your components. A bar tends to have its weight evenly spread across the length of the bar, meaning that for the same weight as a flywheel it'll contain less energy when at full speed. The bar design, though, can attack overhead weapons. Whereas Shunt's axe chopped straight into Hypnodisc's spinner, if it had been Carbide's bar the chances are the axe would have been ripped right off.

So, now we understand the different style of spinner available we can throw something else into the mix. For instance, would you build a horizontal spinner or a vertical one? Again, there isn't a correct answer and teams have been successful worldwide with a variety of spinner types and directions. But what difference does it make having a spinner that spins horizontally or one that spins vertically?

There are two things to think about: impacts and gyroscopic effects. Firstly let's think about big impacts. If you've seen Carbide and Aftershock in battle you may have noticed a difference when the two machines land big impacts on their opponents. When Carbide – the

huge horizontal-bar spinner – hits, both Carbide and its opponent fly apart. This is because the force in Carbide's blade is enough to accelerate both robots away from each other. After each big hit Carbide needs to get back up to speed and resume its attack as quickly as possible. Aftershock, with its vertical disc, is quite different. Because the disc rotates upwards like an upper cutter, when they get a big hit on their opponent although both robots *want* to fly apart Aftershock is planted on the floor. It can't go anywhere. Which means more energy goes into the opponent, making it a bigger hit. It almost has no effect on Aftershock at all. The robot stays in the same spot and can continue its attack, as it famously did against Sabretooth in Series 9, landing one hit directly after another. So this would make it seem like a vertical spinner is better than a horizontal spinner.

When we look at how gyroscopic effects work we can see how our robots might react when the spinners are at full speed. Firstly the vertical spinner. When up to speed the spinning disc will want to maintain its orientation; however, when our robot turns it's trying to change the axis of rotation. This can have a huge effect on the robot and the way it drives. Once up to full speed and trying to turn, the gyroscopic effect in the spinner tries to maintain its axis of rotation while the robot is forcing it to rotate. This results in the robot trying to flip itself over. Robots such as Magnetar and Aftershock show this regularly when in battle. If

↑↑ **Kadeena Machina tears through the gearbox of Dee.**

↑ **Iron-Awe 6 is armed with pneumatically powered side canons for launching entanglement devices at spinners from a distance.**

→ **Aftershock taking chunks out of TERRORHURTZ with his vertical spinner.**

➜ **Pulsar struggles to turn due to the gyroscopic effects of his disc.**

they turn too quickly you see the robot almost levitate as the outside wheel lifts off the ground.

This means the faster a vertical spinner spins, the less agile it is when in close-quarter combat. They literally *can't* turn quickly. By contrast, when a horizontal spinner is up to speed and the robot turns on the spot it doesn't affect the angle of rotation at all, so it has no effect. Where it does play a part, though, is when the horizontal spinner is up to speed and a flipper tries to flip it on to its back. The disc fights to maintain its angle of rotation and actually stops the robot being flipped over. This means that flippers have to slow the disc down if they want to flip the robot on to its back.

Others

This category covers a whole array of creative and whacky weaponry invented by *Robot Wars* competitors. For example, there were the pneumatically powered "petals" used by team Miss Nightshade, an incredible robot that was an entire weapon in itself. When they hit the fire button their entire robot opened up, activating a full 360° axe attack! Next up is the "Meltybrain" robot, as Rory Mangles from Nuts 2 calls his machine. Nuts 2 has two large flails on its sides which are bolted directly to the chassis. On first appearance they look like drag-along ball and chains, which would be of little use. However, when Nuts 2 starts up, it's an incredibly complex and amazing weapon. Nuts 2 spins on the spot, rotating at up to 100 miles per hour. Those ball and chains are now looking pretty dangerous as a weapon, but simply spinning on the spot isn't a good tactic in *Robot Wars* so this is where the clever bit comes in, as Rory explains:

"A 'Meltybrain' controller works by measuring how fast the robot is spinning, and then stopping each motor for a section of the rotation. Repeating this over and over causes the robot to move forward whilst spinning. By having the drive system power the weapon as well, it reduced the cost and made the robot more reliable by having fewer moving parts. It's also a unique system that hasn't been seen on *Robot Wars* before, so we wanted to try it out."

⬆ **Miss Nightshade with 360° axes.**

⬅ **Rory Mangles making tweaks to the software that controls Nuts 2's Melty Brain weapon.**

5
Building a robot safely

Building robots can naturally be very dangerous, so it's vital you take care when in workshop environments. However enthusiastic you may be about getting on with the job in hand, you should always take the time to ensure that your safety isn't put at risk. A moment's lack of attention can result in an accident, as can failure to observe certain elementary precautions.

There'll always be new ways of having accidents, so the following points don't pretend to be a comprehensive list of all the potential dangers. Rather they're intended to make you aware of the more common risks and to encourage a safety-conscious approach to work that you carry out on your robot.

In the workshop

Each year many injuries in engineering workshops are reported to HSE (the Health and Safety Executive). Almost two-thirds of all accidents relate to moving around the workshop. Of these, half are related to lifting and moving goods around while the other half are related to slips, trips and falls. Regardless of the size of space you're building in, whether a workshop, shed or garage, the first important rules are as follows:

- Make sure your space is free of trip hazards and spillages.
- Robot parts can be very heavy. Don't attempt to lift heavy components on your own. Ask someone to help.
- While building your robot you're likely to be using power tools and machinery. It's imperative to ensure under all circumstances that you and others in your workshop are wearing appropriate clothing and personal safety gear.
- Always remove jewellery and wristwatches.
- Keep loose clothing and long hair well out of the way of moving parts or machinery.
- Don't use ill-fitting tools which may slip and cause injury.
- Be aware of tiredness and take regular breaks to keep fresh and energized.
- Don't allow children in the workshop area unattended.
- If you're working alone let somebody know where you are and what you're doing. Ask them to check up on you periodically.
- If, in spite of following these precautions, you're unfortunate enough to injure yourself, seek medical attention as soon as possible.

Testing

Once parts of your robot are complete, it's always a great motivator to test components and see parts moving. At this point, always follow the *Robot Wars* event rules:

- If you're testing locomotion, ensure your robot is on a cradle to raise moving parts off the surface.
- If you're testing parts of weapon systems, only if it's safe to do so, always use your weapon locking bars to ensure components can't move.

- Sharp-edge protection is always important too.
- Robots are very dangerous machines so only power them up and operate them in a safe environment. The best place to test your robot safely is at *Robot Wars* or one of the many live events that take place in arenas around the country. (There may be restrictions in place on your weaponry depending on the level of event safety. Only www.robotwars.tv events are associated with *Robot Wars*.)

Batteries

- Never leave terminals exposed, as they may spark and cause severe burns.
- When using lithium batteries always store them in the correct type of lithium sacks.
- Always use the correct type of charger for your batteries.
- Be aware of your batteries' charging limits. Never charge batteries faster than the manufacturer recommends.
- Never leave batteries on charge unattended.
- Always follow the *Robot Wars* rules.

Pneumatics

- Always wear the appropriate personal protective equipment when working on pneumatic systems.
- Never exceed the maximum pressure of your components.
- Follow the *Robot Wars* build rules to ensure you have all the safety components correctly installed in your system before attempting to operate anything.
- Don't pressurize any systems until all of the connections have been completed and secured.
- Ensure your system fully complies with the *Robot Wars* pneumatics rules before testing,

to ensure all safety components required are in the system.
- Don't disconnect any components or piping while under pressure.
- There is danger of injury when switching compressed air on! Cylinders may extend or retract automatically depending on your system design.
- Use the shortest possible piping between components.
- Always wear safety glasses when pressurizing systems.
- Ensure the system is depressurized before attempting to dismantle any part of it.

Hydraulics

- Always wear the appropriate personal protective equipment when working on hydraulic systems.
- Follow the *Robot Wars* build rules to ensure you have all the safety components correctly installed in your system before attempting to operate anything.
- Hydraulic oil is extremely slippery. Ensure spills are thoroughly cleaned up immediately.
- Ensure you never exceed the manufacturers' pressure ratings of your components.
- Ensure all connections and components are correctly fitted.

- If you have a leak in your system never use your hand to locate it. High-pressure oil released through a leak can penetrate skin or eyes, causing severe injury.
- Ensure your system isn't pressurized before disconnecting components and hoses.
- Ensure you have precautions in place to contain oil leaks when disconnecting components.
- Be aware that hydraulic oil can be extremely hot, so let your system cool before disconnecting components.

Robot Wars safety rules: how to fight a battle safely

Naturally, safety during *Robot Wars* is critical and follows stringent procedures to ensure that operating robots is done in a safe and sound manner and only under very specific circumstances. Teams can't just turn up and play – there's a specific process that must be followed. On arrival at a *Robot Wars* event teams must sign in and await their pit bench allocation. From this point on the event rules are already enforced. There are a number of cardinal rules that teams *must* adhere to whilst in the pits area working on their robots. The three main robot-specific rules are:

- **Activation** – proper activation and deactivation of robots is critical. Robots should only be activated in the arena or testing areas with expressed consent of *Robot Wars* and its safety officials. All activation and de-activation of robots must be completed from outside the arena barrier or within specially designated areas.
- **Weapon restraints** – all robots not in an arena or official testing area should have secure safety covers over any sharp edges and restraints on any active weapons or pinch hazards.
- **Carrying cradles** – all robots not in an arena or official testing area should be raised on their carrying cradles in a manner so that their motive power cannot cause movement if the robot were turned on, or cannot roll or fall off the pit tables.

These and other rules must be strictly followed at all times once your team is set up on its pit bench right up until the end of filming. They ensure the robot is physically safe whilst in the pits. The robot can't roll off the pit bench, weapons can't activate and sharp-edge protection must be in place to minimize cuts and injuries whilst working on the robot. This is just the beginning, though. Before any robot is signed off as ready for battle every team must successfully complete their Technical Checks. These Technical Checks are where our technical team take a detailed look at the robot, both inside and out, to check it fully complies with all of *Robot Wars*' build and health and safety rules. These cover everything from checking your battery chargers are the right ones for the batteries you're using to making sure terminals and wiring are properly insulated. One of the critical tests is on the failsafes, which are covered by the following rule.

Dangerous systems

All systems that are deemed to be "dangerous" (normally the drive and weapons) must have a "failsafe" device. This MUST bring the systems to a preset "off" or "zero" position if the transmitter signal experiences interference or is lost. These devices should also failsafe when the receiver battery is low or if power is completely lost.

During these checks teams must also pass a functionality test to ensure the robot performs correctly inside the *Robot Wars* test arena. This includes checking the drive systems function can be controlled correctly, as well as specific weapon tests to check for functionality and safety. Once all the checks are signed off you're given the green light to battle. Don't forget, though, that if your robot has taken severe damage during the competition it may need to go through another Technical Check before it's permitted to continue battling.

Once they've passed the critical Technical Checks most teams breathe a sigh of relief, and it's time to prepare for battle. You'll soon be told who your opponent(s) are, which may mean you'll need to make some modifications if you have interchangeable parts; otherwise its strap your batteries in and make your final checks before heading up to the arena. Getting up to it entails your robot being put on a hydraulic trolley that's used to lift it to arena height. Your robot must remain in its cradle at all times to prevent it rolling off.

Once you've arrived behind the audience seating you'll meet one of the Arena Marshals, who'll stay with you until the arena is locked and you're ready for battle. Your robot is now transferred from the trolley to the catwalk that leads between the audience seating, through the arena doors and into the inner arena. The inner arena walls will currently be lowered so the robots can be pushed into position in front of the lowered barriers. From here you're under the instruction of the Arena Marshals and Event Manager. The audience will have seen your machine and will no doubt be excited and cheering, but it's important for you to remain focused.

At this point the walls raise to create an enclosed environment that contains the robots. From here you wait for the instruction to arm up your robot. All robots in the arena are risk assessed and armed in reverse order, with the fastest weapons or robots left until last. When, and only when, you're instructed to do so, you may arm your robot under an Arena Marshal's supervision. All weapon locking bars remain in place and are only removed once the arena is ready to be locked. Once they're active and you're happy the robot is ready you're taken from the arena and led up to the control booths from where you can oversee the action.

There must be no movement of robots whatsoever until the arena doors are locked. You may notice the Arena Marshals are still in the arena, arming other robots or waiting for the all-clear to remove weapon locking bars. As soon as the locking bars are removed, the arena is cleared and the doors locked. It's time for battle!

All sorts of carnage can happen during a battle. It can be total chaos and completely unpredictable. Nevertheless, the Arena Marshals are on constant watch throughout each fight, assessing how damaged robots are after big impacts and judging how much a robot's functionality may have been compromised. They're

assessing the structural integrity of the robots too. Are the weapons or chassis compromised to a point where the robot may not hold together if the weapon fired while being disarmed? Does a team still have control of their robot? There's a lot to think about, especially with multiple robots in the battle or if a robot has been flipped out of the arena.

Once "cease" has been called the roboteers stay in their booths while the Arena Marshals make the robots safe. They're the only people allowed in the arena until all robots are fully deactivated and any further risks, such as fires, are dealt with. Once the arena has been made safe the robots are brought out through the central catwalk to be reunited with their teams. Though they may be disarmed and their weapon restraints back in position they remain dangerous to handle. It's likely armor has been gouged or ripped, which naturally can cause injuries when working on the robot, so it's vital that teams keep their robot on the cradle, ensure sharp edge protection is back in position and take extra care when handling their machine.

↓ **An Arena Marshal wears appropriate safety clothing as a robot is disarmed.**

6

Build your own robot

Design

Designing a robot can be daunting. Not knowing where to start or trying to come up with unique designs often leads to ideas that never make it into reality.

The biggest question is "What do you want your robot to do?" Do you want to flip things out of the arena, create huge sparks from spinning weapons, grab hold of robots to take control in the arena or simply beat them with a huge hammer?

There is no perfect type of design in *Robot Wars* – a robot's strength against one opponent will be its weakness against another, so thought must go into deciding if you want to concentrate your best efforts on your weapon or the armor, or where you can make compromises to minimize your weaknesses.

Sam Smith and Dave Moulds – Team Carbide

" One of the keys to building a successful machine is in making the right design trade-offs and using the available weight in the areas which make the robot most competitive. The philosophy behind Carbide wasn't just to build a destructive spinning weapon but also to avoid compromising too much on the drive system, chassis or armor so that we could drive the weapon effectively to the opposition and take a hit or two without breaking. For example, we could have made Carbide's weapon much more powerful, but to meet the weight limit it would have had to be fitted with light armor, potentially making it easy to beat by a lucky hit from an opponent or House Robot. The combat strategy for Carbide doesn't really involve using the House Robots or hazards to our advantage as some teams do, but we do tend to take care to avoid the Pit and low-sided sections of the arena walls that could result in a quick loss.

"It's great winning *Robot Wars*, but for us the challenge of getting to the top and seeing our machine perform as intended is what appeals most. The battle-testing of Series 8 highlighted a few areas of the machine that could be improved and optimized to make it more reliable and more powerful. Those upgrades worked faultlessly for Series 9, leading to our dominating run to the final. During Series 3 Carbide experienced some new technical failures that showed just how close to the edge those parts were operating. But once again it helps us to evolve the machine and go on to improve its resilience in future. "

Understanding the weapon type you want on a robot early on really helps, as it will help to clarify your ideas and help you find inspiration for the design. Not all robots need a theme or style, as that can develop as the design progresses. Apollo is a key example of a robot built simply around its huge weapon, with no compromise for aesthetics. Razer, on the other hand, was built with a theme and character in mind, which was hand-sculpted into the most recognizable robot ever to appear on *Robot Wars*. It's really helpful to create a "mood board" of images that give you inspiration for your design. Whether it be other robots, shapes or characters, having something to look at while designing can help keep you on track with what you're trying to achieve.

Budgets are a big factor to consider before you get too far into the design process. Robots can be built for almost nothing or up to tens of thousands of dollars. The great thing about *Robot Wars* is that money doesn't make the best machines. It's all about the designs! Money helps to have spares and fancier equipment, but robots such as Razer have shown that buying used and industrial-type components rather than high-tech products and materials can still make you the most successful robot in *Robot Wars* history. Sourcing materials and components cheap isn't too hard if you know the right places to look. Offcuts of Hardox, titanium, aluminium and other materials can be found cheaply at scrapyards or fabrication companies, particularly places that repair agricultural equipment like digger buckets. eBay is also a great source for motors and materials.

Every component must be thought out and decided on, whether for the weapons, the drive or anything else required to make the robot run. It's critical to know what parts you'll be using before you start building a chassis, as trying to fit in components after it's built can be very difficult, leading to big design changes halfway through. Components can be laid out in CAD, with a rough weapon layout to start working out where things will best fit together. It's at this stage that the shape of the machine

→ **It doesn't look a lot like Shunt yet.**

is dictated, so ideally a lot of time needs to be spent on it.

A lot of people don't like to use CAD modelling software and instead use original CAD – cardboard-aided design! The design process for the new House Robots relied on a mix of the two, because sometimes looking at a computer screen for the entire design can make it difficult to understand the scale and feel of a more organic-looking robot. With Shunt we knew the weapons we needed and a rough style, but from there we had a clean slate to really push the boundaries. We worked out the components we needed to give him a big increase in power and performance, and physically laid them out to start with to get a mental idea of how it was all going to fit together.

This provided some rough dimensions to start designing sections of the robot using AutoDesk Fusion 360. The buckets were made in wood and cardboard and used to help finalize the layout. When we were confident of this we designed more sections in Fusion 360 and accurately manufactured them, adding to the robot along the way. Even the body shape was drawn and cut out by hand so that we could step back and tweak the design. The positions of the front and rear buckets were constantly changed until they were just right, and we mounted them permanently.

↑ **First mock-up of the bucket. It looks huge!**

↓ **The axe looks powerful.**

↓ **Shunt is coming to life now.**

Project 1 - Bug Bot

Materials required

All parts available from robot parts suppliers and high-street electrical stores

- 2 x 30 mm elastic bands
- 2 x geared motors
- 2 x micro switches
- 1 x battery holder
- 2 x plastic wheels
- 1 x rocker switch
- 2 x cable ties, 203 mm long and 4.5 mm wide
- 100 mm of black wire
- 400 mm of red wire
- 4 x AA batteries
- 1 piece of card approximately 175 mm x 150 mm, maximum 3 mm thick
- 1 x 3D printable Bug Bot body

Tools required

- Soldering iron and solder
- Scissors
- Double-sided tape
- Hot-melt glue gun and glue
- Wire strippers

Bug Bot is a great starter project, being really easy to build by anyone interested in building their first robot. He's a simple "object avoidance robot," and with minimal tools yours should be up and running within just a few hours! Then just switch him on and watch him drive about using his antennas to detect and avoid objects.

In this project we'll be using micro switches to cut the power to the drive motors, which will enable the robot to turn out of the way of objects. By the end of this guide you'll also have learned how to solder.

1

Before you start, ensure the surface where you're working is clean and clear and that the surface is protected against damage. Use a hobby mat or cutting board to work on. Make sure you have all your components and tools and you're ready to start.

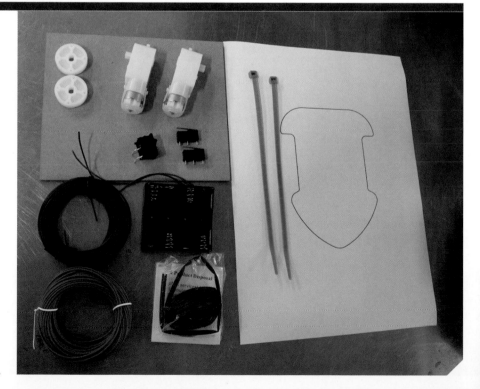

➔ **The components.**

2

- Your first step is to cut out Bug Bot's base. Photocopy the Bug Bot base layout on page 78 or draw around it with tracing paper.
- Cut out the paper base using scissors. You'll now use this as your template.
- Take your card and lay the template on top. Using a marker, carefully draw around the template and cut out the cardboard Bug Bot base. Make sure you keep the template, as this also shows the positioning for the components. If you have a laser cutter, you can download the drawings from www.robotwars.tv and cut them out directly.

→ **Creating the base template.**

3

- Now you have your base you need to lay out Bug Bot's components as per the template. This is a good check to ensure that everything fits where it should and that you haven't made any mistakes.
- While the components are neatly laid out let's take a look at how the Bug Bot works. He has two drive motors, a battery pack and two micro switches. The battery power runs through the switches at the front and then goes to the opposite motor. When Bug Bot is switched on the motors drive him until one of the switches is pressed and cuts power to the opposite motor. This causes the robot to turn away from the object. Simple!

→ **The Bug Bot component layout.**

4

- The rocker switch is the main power switch for your robot and battery pack. Using the hot-melt glue gun, glue it to the underside of the battery pack. Be careful when using the glue as it remains very hot for a period of time after use.

→ **The switch attached to the battery box.**

- With the components laid out in position on the base, you need to cut the correct lengths of wire and prepare them for soldering. Cut one piece of black wire 60 millimeters long, one piece of red wire 50 millimeters long and three pieces of red wire 120 millimeters long.
- Strip both ends of the wire insulation to expose approximately 4 millimeters of the internal wire.
- Take the battery pack and strip the ends of the red wires and the black wire.
- You're now ready to "tin" the wires and components, so let's learn how to solder! Whatever you intend to solder, you should tin both ends before you attempt to solder them together. This coats or fills the wires and components with solder so that you can easily melt them together.
- Be very careful when soldering. The iron and components get extremely hot, so never leave them unaccompanied and always switch them off as soon as you're finished.
- Plug in your soldering iron and wait for it to heat up.
- Once up to temperature take the iron and hold it like a pen.
- Heat the wire/component with the tip for a few seconds. Don't heat the solder directly.
- Keeping the iron tip on the component, bring the solder to the heated wire. The solder

↓ **Tinning the wires.**

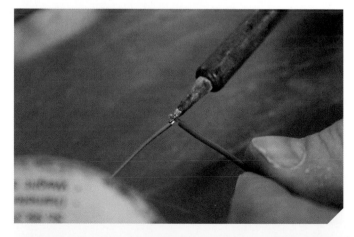

will flow into and around the heated wire/component.
- Remove the solder when you have enough solder on the wire/component, then remove the iron tip.
- Keep the wire/component still until the solder has fully cooled and solidified.
- You've now "tinned" all your wires and components where the wires need to attach. Now it's time to solder the wires to the components to create the circuit.
- To solder the wires to the components, bring the tinned wire to the tinned component and hold them together.
- Bring the tip of the iron to the wire and hold it there until the iron has melted the solder on both the wire and the component.
- Take the iron away from the joint and hold the joint still until the solder cools and solidifies. You should now have a solid connection.
- Now that you know how to solder your connections it's time to get the wires soldered.
- Firstly make sure your components are laid out correctly. Then take the battery pack with the switch attached. The red wire on the battery pack will be soldered to one of the tabs on the switch leaving the black wire left on the battery pack.
- Next, ensure the micro switches are laid out in the correct orientation as per the picture opposite. Then take the small 50-millimeter length of red wire and solder each end to the inside tab on both of the micro switches.
- Take the three 120-millimeter-long red wires. Solder the first wire to the outside tab on the left micro switch. Solder the second wire to the outside tab on the right-hand micro switch. Finally the third wire should be soldered to the inner tab, along with the short wire, on the right-hand micro switch.
- You should now have the two micro switches soldered together by the smallest red wire, with three long red wires lying down the middle of the base.
- You now need to connect the opposite end of the three red wires to their components. Take the middle wire and the battery pack.

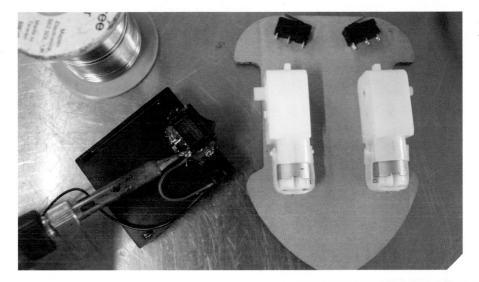

← Positive soldered to the switch.

↓ Micro switches with wires.

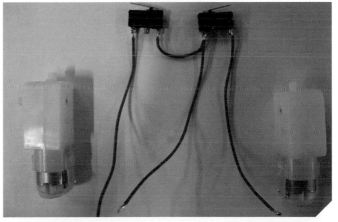

This wire needs to be soldered to the next tab on the switch.

- The remaining two red wires need to be connected to the motors. It's important to attach the correct wire to the correct tab on the motors, otherwise your bug will drive backwards or switch off the wrong motor when the antenna is pushed.

- With the motors in position, as per the images on the right, take the wire connected to the LEFT micro switch and solder it to the BOTTOM tab on the RIGHT-hand motor.

- Next, take the wire on the RIGHT micro switch and solder it to the BOTTOM tab on the LEFT-hand motor. The two red motor wires should be crossing over in the middle.

- Now you need to solder the negative side of the battery pack to the top tab on the left-hand motor.

- Finally, take the small black wire and solder each end to the top tab on both the left-hand and right-hand motors.

- Your Bug Bot is now all wired up and ready to test.

- You can now add the batteries to the battery pack. Switch on your Bug Bot and both motors should now rotate. Try pressing the switches on the front of the robot and notice how the opposite motor switches off.

→ Positive side of the circuit complete.

6

- You're now ready to start attaching your components to the cardboard base.
- Use the double-sided tape to attach the two drive motors firmly to the base. Ensure they line up accurately with the base drawing provided on the template.

→ **Soldering complete and ready for a test.**

7

- Cut two small strips of double-sided tape and stick the two micro switches to the base. Again ensure they're the correct orientation and angle to ensure the antennas' best performance.

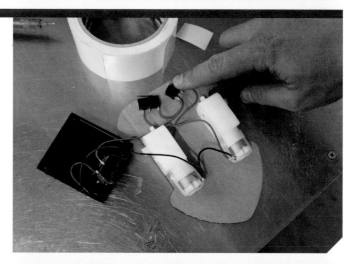

→ **Attaching the motors and switches to the base.**

8

- Add two strips of double-sided tape to the bottom side of the battery pack, either side of the rocker switch. The battery pack will now sit on top of the drive motors as per the images on the right. Take care when positioning the battery pack to ensure it's located centrally on the motors.

→ **All components in place.**

9

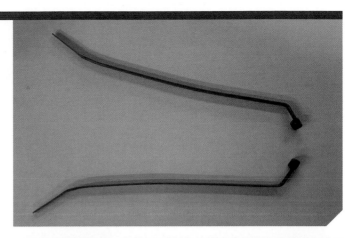

- Now it's time to add the antennas. For this you'll be using the cable ties, as they're nice and flexible, lightweight, and will provide your robot with good reach. The first thing you need to do is bend the cable tie to create a good antenna shape.
- Taking the end with the ratchet in it (the plastic square you normally feed the cable tie back through), make a 45° bend approximately 15 millimeters from the end.
- Now flex the tip of the cable tie in the opposite direction as per the image on the right.

➔ **Cable ties formed to create antenna shape.**

10

- You now need to attach the cable ties accurately to the micro switches. Use the hot-glue gun again to add a small strip of glue to the metal levers.
- Add the cable tie end to the micro switch and hold it in place until the hot glue cools and solidifies. Make sure you take extra care to keep the antennas level, and glue on only one antenna at a time to avoid the glue cooling too quickly on the second one.

➔ **Attaching the cable ties to the micro switches.**

11

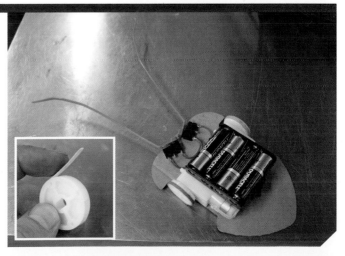

- Before you can test your Bug Bot properly you need to add the wheels and tires. For this you need to use the two elastic bands on the plastic wheels to give Bug Bot extra grip.
- Cut thin strips of double-sided tape and wrap them around the circumference of each wheel.
- Carefully add the elastic bands to the wheels before pushing the wheels on to the motor shaft.
- Finally, secure the wheels to the motors with the screws provided with the wheels.

➔ **The Bug Bot complete and ready to test.**

12

→ **Ready to scurry!**

■ Now your Bug Bot should be fully operational and ready to go. However, you could make it look amazing first. For this we've designed your Bug Bot its very own 3D printable body shell – just download the Bug Bot Shell file from www.robotwars.tv.

■ If you have access to a 3D printer you're ready to print and attach. If you don't have access to a printer, but would like to have a shell made, a search online, or in a local services directory, should enable you to find a suitable and affordable 3D printing supplier.

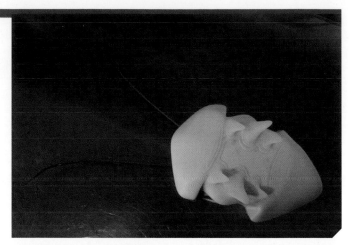

Congratulations! Your Bug Bot is now complete and ready to test. He'll operate best on flat, smooth surfaces. Try placing a number of food tins on the floor, switch on your Bug Bot and watch how he navigates his way through the obstacles. You could try bending the antennas into new shapes to see how this affects his performance. Let us know how your project goes by tweeting the hashtag #RWBugBot.

Now that your first project is complete you're ready to build your first fully remote-controlled combat robot.

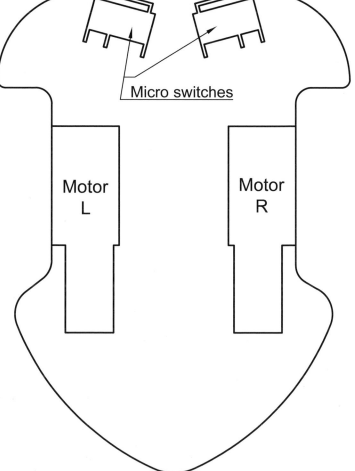

Micro switches

Motor L

Motor R

→ **Bug Bot base layout.**

Project 2 – Flip Bot

Flip Bot is an exciting project that can easily be made at home over two weekends. It's a two-wheel-drive combat robot armed with a powerful lifting arm designed to flip over its opponents. Despite being a fully functional remote-controlled robot it's very easy to make, as you'll be using inexpensive resources. The drive motors and batteries come from cordless drills and the chassis is made from MDF or aluminium, both of which are easy to cut at home with a jigsaw. This project will delve into the practicalities of how combat robots work, and you'll learn all about the electronics and remote-control elements as Flip Bot comes together.

Tools required

- Soldering iron and solder
- Scissors
- Double-sided tape
- Jigsaw with aluminium cutting blade
- Cordless drill and drill bits
- Wire strippers
- Crimp tool
- 7 mm, 10 mm and 13 mm spanners
- Set of Allen keys
- Torx driver

Materials required

- 2 mm–3 mm aluminium sheet
- 2 x cordless drills
- 1 x radio gear (Part No Spektrum DX6E or similar from any reasonable model shop)
- 1 x dual motor speed controller (available from robot part suppliers and model shops)
- 1 x dual RC switch (available from robot part suppliers and model shops)
- 6 x 200 mm circumference jubilee clips
- 1 pair of EC5 connectors
- 2 pairs of 4 mm bullet connectors
- 1 pack of 20 x 25 mm angle braces
- 1 x 100 mm hinge
- 1 x linear actuator (Part No GLA2000 with 100 mm stroke from www.gimsonrobotics.co.uk)
- 2 x steel actuator brackets (from www.gimsonrobotics.co.uk)
- 2 m of red wire
- 1 m of black wire
- 1 x 250 mm long Velcro strap
- 2 x 100 mm wheels

40 x M4 x 15 mm dome head bolts	4 x M8 x 20 mm dome head bolts
40 x M4 lock nuts	4 x M8 lock nuts
80 x M4 washers	8 x M8 washers
8 x M6 x 20mm dome head bolts	2 x M8 x 60 mm dome head bolts
8 x M6 lock nuts	2 x M8 lock nuts
16 x M6 washers	4 x M8 washers

1

Before you start, as per the Bug Bot project you need to ensure that the surface where you're working is clean and clear. To ensure the surface is protected against damage, use a hobby mat or cutting board to work on. Make sure you have all your components and tools and you're ready to start.

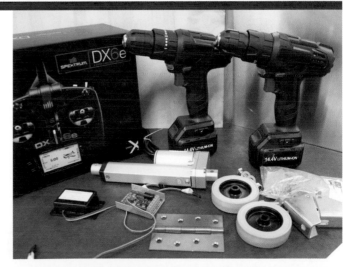

➜ Flip Bot components.

- Flip Bot was designed in CAD (computer aided design) using Autodesk Fusion 360. The first step in constructing him is to make his body work. Head to www.robotwars.tv, where you can download all of the technical drawings in the form of PDFs or DXFs.
- If you're cutting the robot out with a jigsaw yourself, download each of the PDFs and print them out at full size. As the parts are larger than an A4 piece of paper, once they're printed you need to line up the edges and use tape to stick the sheets together accurately. That way you have all the components printed to full size and ready to use as templates.
- To save space, cut around the outside edge of each printed component with scissors, leaving 10 millimeters around the black lines.
- Next, get your sheet of aluminium and lay out each component one at a time. Using double-sided tape stick the paper templates down to the metal surface.
- With the templates securely attached, use a jigsaw to carefully cut out each component, one piece at a time.
- Once all the components are cut, and with the templates still in place, use a center punch to mark the holes and slots.
- Once all the holes and slots are marked out, carefully drill the holes with a cordless drill, following the hole sizes on the templates. For the slots you should drill several holes along their length and then carefully use a jigsaw or a file to clean up each slot.
- Once all the components are cut out and the holes drilled in position, use a file to remove any burrs and clean up the edges of each part.
- If you intend to use a machine or you're asking a company to cut out your components, Step 2 becomes much easier! Simply download the DXF files. These can then be sent directly to a company to cut the components out of the desired material and mail them back to you.

↓ **Finished metal parts cut and drilled.**

3

- Now all the panels are cut and prepared you can start to assemble the chassis. The main component, to which everything else attaches, is the base plate. The first panel that needs to be attached to it is the rear plate.
- Use two 25 millimeter angle braces along with the M4 bolts, a washer on both sides and the lock nuts to secure the rear plate in place.

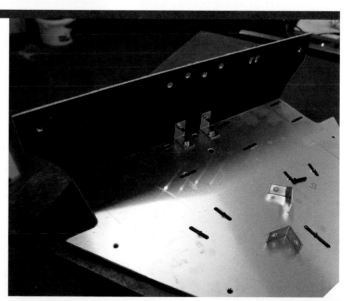

→ **Rear panel bolted in place.**

4

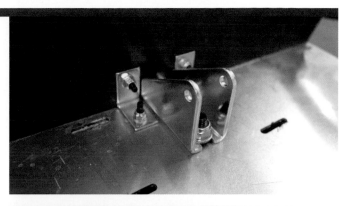

■ With the rear panel in position it's time to attach the first bracket, which will allow the linear actuator to pivot on the base. The actuator will power your weapon, so the first bracket will attach to the base plate between the two angle pieces mounting the rear panel.

■ The second actuator bracket will attach to the flipper arm later in the build. Use the M8 bolts with washers either side and the M8 lock nuts.

➔ **Actuator bracket bolted to the base plate.**

5

■ Once the actuator bracket is in place the next step is to prepare the side armor panels for mounting to the chassis. To do this you need to add the desired bends in the armor to match the base plate. On the template use the dotted lines as the bend lines to ensure the folds are in the correct position. Take care to accurately bend the armor panels a little at a time. Periodically use the side of the base plate as a jig to check the correct angle has been achieved.

➔ **Side armor with bends that match the base plate.**

6

■ Now that both side armor panels are the correct shape and match the base plate you need to bolt them down. Use six angle brackets to bolt both side armor panels to the base plate and a further two to secure both side panels to the rear panel.

■ You can add a piece of plastic on the front bolts underneath the robot, which will act as a skid for the robot to drive on.

■ To ensure you get the best fit when bolting down a panel which has multiple bolts, don't tighten up the first bolt. Instead fit all the nuts and bolts so that they're slightly loose. Then once they're all in place go around again and tighten them up. This helps to align the bolts and keep everything square.

➔ **Both side armor panels bolted to the chassis.**

7

■ Using the pins provided with the actuator brackets, attach the base of the linear actuator to the mounting bracket. Ensure the motor of the actuator is towards the center of the robot.

■ Make sure each pin is secure using the R clip provided.

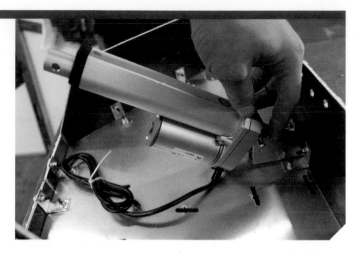

→ **Actuator mounted to the bracket.**

8

■ The next step is to modify the cordless drills to use as your drive motors. Drill motors are perfect for robots up to the featherweight class, because these mass-produced motors come with compact lightweight gearboxes. Drill motors are also very easy to buy from any hardware store and, relative to purpose-made robotics motors with seven gearboxes, are very affordable. The other benefit for our project is that we can use the lightweight lithium ion battery packs that come with a cordless drill along with the charger, meaning we don't have to buy these separately.

■ Take both cordless drills and set the batteries aside. These particular drills have screws holding the plastic body together with Torx heads.

■ Remove all nine screws in each drill and carefully open the plastic body. Keep the screws safe, as you'll need to reassemble the body later.

→ **Opening the cordless drills.**

9

- Now that the drill motor is exposed, carefully remove the battery connector, LED and trigger from the plastic body but keep the motor in position.
- Cut the wires from the motor to the trigger as close to the trigger as possible.
- Cut the wires from the battery connector again as close to the trigger as possible. The trigger and LED can now be discarded. Keep hold of the battery connector as you'll use this in your robot later.

→ **Removing the trigger.**

10

- With just the motor left in the drill's plastic case it's almost time to reconnect the body. Firstly you need to make a hole in the plastic casing to allow the motor wires to go through it. Take the empty half of the drill case and cut out the semi-circle in the rear section.

→ **Cut-out in the plastic drill body.**

11

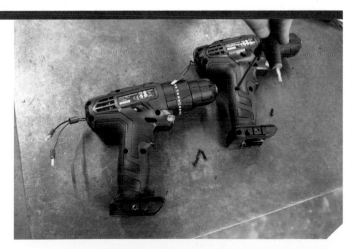

- Reassemble the plastic bodies of both drills using the original Torx screws. Ensure the motor wires are carefully positioned so that they protrude out of the rear of the plastic drill case.
- With the wires exposed, add the male bullet connectors to both the black and red motor wires using a crimping tool.

→ **Modified drill motors complete and ready to use for drive motors.**

12

■ With the cordless drills modified and ready you can now install them into the chassis. Using three jubilee clips per motor, secure the motors in place by looping the jubilee clips through the slots in the chassis. Ensure the drills are parallel before tightening the clips.

■ Tighten the clip closest to the actuator first, again not too tightly to allow the drill a little movement.

■ Then properly secure the handle of the drill and, finally, the jubilee clip closest to the drill chuck.

↗→ **Drive motors mounted in the chassis.**

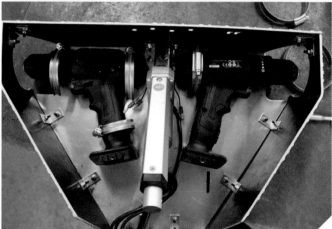

13

■ The next step is to add the hinge to the rear panel of your robot. Using the M6 bolts with washers either side and lock nuts, bolt the hinge to the inner side of the robot.

14

■ You're now ready to start assembling the flipper. The first task is to fold the flipper arm to fit the flipper supports. Using the lines on the template, carefully bend the flipper plate whilst periodically offering it up to the flipper supports to check the correct angle is achieved. Take care to add the bend in the correct direction by ensuring the holes for mounting the plate to the hinge are the correct way around. These are not symmetrical, so if this isn't checked the flipper won't fit the robot.

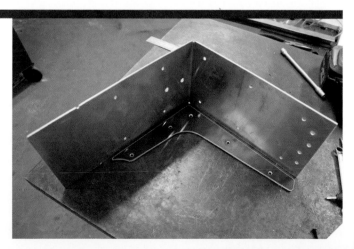

→ **Flipper plate bent to match flipper side supports.**

15

■ With the flipper plate correctly bent to fit the side supports, you now need to use ten of the angle brackets and the M4 bolts to attach both side supports to the flipper plate. Take care to keep the flipper square and straight when fitting these, as it's possible to add a twist to the frame if it isn't done correctly.

↗→ Flipper assembled.

16

■ Attach the second actuator bracket to the underside of the flipper arm using two M8 bolts. Be careful with the orientation. The hole for the actuator is closest to the corner of the flipper.

■ Using the template provided add a bend of approximately 45° to the flipper tip. This can be modified later to suit how close to the floor you'd like your flipper to run.

↓ Actuator mount attached and the flipper tip is bent into shape.

17

■ Now the flipper arm is assembled you can attach it to the robot. Firstly use the M6 bolts to bolt the rear of the flipper arm to the hinge.

■ Once in position use the second pin provided with the actuator mount to attach the actuator to the flipper arm. Secure the pin with the R clip provided. A tip is to use a battery to extend the actuator to make attaching the flipper arm to the robot as easy as possible.

→ The flipper arm attached to the robot.

18

- Flip Bot is now mechanically almost finished, so it's time to add the electronics. Firstly you need to make a simple wiring loom that incorporates the battery connector from the cordless drill and your removable safety link.
- Cut two 450-millimeter lengths of the red wire. The first wire should have one end soldered into one half of the EC5 connector and the other end stripped to expose 5 millimeters of wire. The second wire should have one end soldered into the second half of the EC5 connector and the other end soldered on to the cordless drill battery connector to replace the existing red wire.
- Cut a black wire 150 millimeters long and solder one end on to the negative side of the drill battery connector, replacing the existing one. The other end can be stripped to expose the wire.
- Finally, to make the safety link take a 100-millimeter length of black wire and solder both ends as a loop into the remaining EC5 connector.

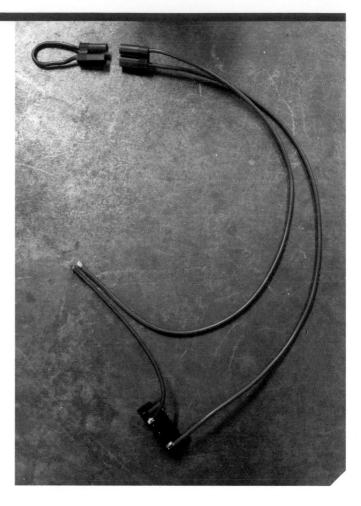

→ **Removable link and battery connector wiring loom.**

- Take the receiver from the radio gear set, the Sabertooth motor controller and the RC relay. Add double-sided tape to the rear and carefully position them on to the base as per the base plate template below.

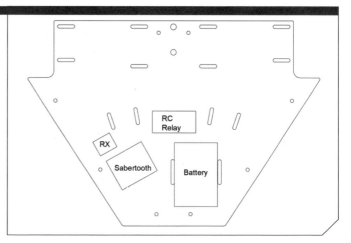

→ **Layout for the electronic components.**

- With the components now all in position you need to complete the wiring. First you need to connect the receiver to the motor controller and RC relay using the small servo leads with three wires each. On the motor controller take Ch1 (FWD) and plug it into Ele (Elevator) in the receiver. Ch2 (turn) needs to plug into Ail (Aileron) on the receiver. The servo lead on the RC relay plugs into Rud (rudder) in the receiver.
- Now the long red wire coming from the removable link needs to be connected into the B+ screw terminal on the motor controller. The negative wire from the battery terminal needs to be screwed into the B- terminal.
- Next cut two red and two black wires each 200 millimeters long and strip both ends on all of them. Screw the two red wires into terminals 1A and 2A. The two black wires should be screwed into terminals 1B and 2B.
- On the opposite ends of these red and black wires a female bullet connector should be attached with the crimping tool. These red and black wires can now be connected to the corresponding drive motors as per the image above right.
- You can now wire up the RC relay to control the linear actuator for the weapon. Start by shortening the wires on the actuator to 250 millimeters and strip both ends to expose the wire. Following the wiring diagram on the right, continue to wire up the RC relay.

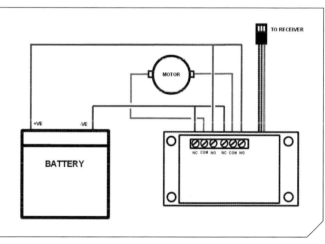

21

- Use the slots on the rear panel to securely mount the removable link with cable ties.

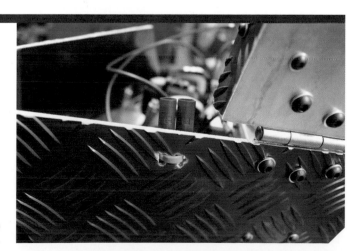

→ **The removable link secured to the rear panel.**

22

■ Before you're ready for a dry test you need to set up the motor controller to ensure you get the correct performance and configuration. The controller can be programmed via the dip switches on the board. You want to enable mixed mode, enable exponential for smoother operating at low speeds, select lithium mode, disable ramping and disable auto calibrate.

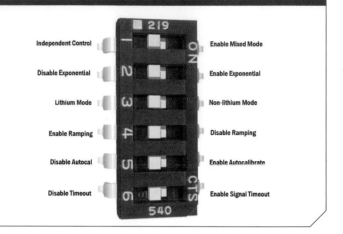

→ **Dip-switch settings.**

23

■ Using the Velcro strap, secure the drill battery to the chassis through the slots in the base. The battery connector can now be connected to the battery. The robot won't power up until the removable link is in position.

■ While the wheels still aren't attached now is a good time to power up the robot and test the functions. Ensure the robot is stable and that you're out of the way of the actuator. Despite being a relatively small robot it still packs a lot of power in the lifter so ensure you keep clear of this at all times.

■ When you're ready, power up the transmitter then the robot by inserting the removable link. The right-hand stick will power your drive motors. Check that forwards, backwards, left and right are correct.

■ Next you can test the lifter. Left and right on the left stick will raise and lower the flipper. Remove the link once you've finished testing. Be very careful when operating the robot as the motors are powerful enough to cause harm. Only test a robot's functionality when it's safe to do so and *never* when you're on your own.

→ **The battery is secured to the base with the Velcro strap.**

All you need to do to complete your robot is add the wheels. Using the long M8 bolts, tightly clamp each wheel between two washers and a lock nut. With both wheels attached to the long bolts these can be inserted into the chuck on the drive motors.

→ **One wheel secured to the bolt.**

Congratulations, your Flip Bot is now ready for battle! He'll operate best on a smooth, flat floor. The high-power flipper is more than a match for his opponents and can easily lift his own weight. If he's flipped over, raising the arm to the top will roll him on to his back. From here driving will ensure Flip Bot lands on his wheels. Don't forget that with the robot having two drive motors you'll have a spare battery to keep on battling. From this point on you can modify Flip Bot by adding top armor or maybe trying different wheels. If you make this project tag photos with #RWFlipBot to show us your progress.

⬇ **Flip Bot ready for battle!**

Project 3 - a fully controllable *Robot Wars* challenger

→ Challenger side view.

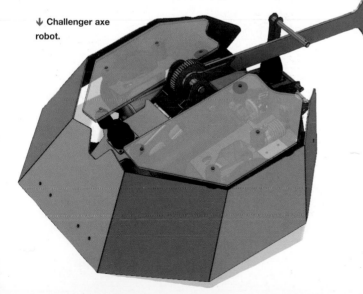

↓ Challenger axe robot.

If you've ever dreamed of building a *Robot Wars* contender but not known where to start, or are building a robot already and want to learn more, this section is the one for you. Here we'll be designing and building a heavyweight competition robot, built to conform to the current rules at the time of writing and ready to fight in *Robot Wars*. Everyone designs robots differently, and there's no right or wrong way to create your own machine, so we aim to show you a range of techniques used for

designing featherweight robots all the way up to designing the mighty House Robots.

The first thing to consider is what sort of robot you want. This will usually revolve around the weapon you want to use and the arenas you'll be using it in. For this example, we've chosen to build an axe-armed robot – a powerful weapon with a good nimble drive system, armor that can stand up to some of the best machines and, best of all, one that can be safely used and tested at live events, as well as in *Robots Wars* on TV!

Tools required

Welder	Flat file
Hammer	Clamps
Pillar drill	Soldering iron
4.5 mm drill	(minimum 60W)
8.5 mm drill	Solder
10.5 mm drill	Wire cutters
M10 tap	Wire strippers
Vice	Pneumatic pipe
Angle grinder	cutter
Ratchet spanner	Small flat-blade
set	screwdriver
Adjustable	Rule/tape
spanner	measure
Allen keys	Lathe, or access
(full set)	to a lathe
Round file	Hacksaw

Materials required

- 3 mm Hardox 1,200 mm x 1,000 mm
- 4 mm Hardox 1,220 mm x 1,500 mm
- 10 mm Hardox 800 mm x 430 mm
- 3 mm aluminium plate 140 mm x 90 mm
- 25 mm diameter ground steel bar 310 mm long
- 12 mm diameter ground steel bar 145 mm long
- 30 mm diameter x 2 mm thick wall steel tube 100 mm long
- 20 mm diameter steel tube 400 mm long
- 10 mm polycarbonate sheet 600 mm x 650 mm
- 6 x 60 mm diameter x 35 mm M10 rubber mounts (male to female)
- 8 x 50 mm diameter x 45 mm M10 rubber mounts (male to female)
- 4 x 20 mm diameter x 15 mm M6 rubber mounts (male to female)
- 8 x 40 mm diameter x 15 mm M10 rubber mounts (male to female)
- 2 x rubber bump stops RS part No 408-8199
- 2.5MOD 52-tooth steel gear with 25 mm bore and no hub
- 2.5MOD round rack 500 mm long
- Selection of nuts and bolts and washer, M3-M10
- 6 x 4 mm diameter x 40 mm split pins
- 25 mm ID track roller bearing, LFR5206-25
- 50 mm hard foam 200 mm x 150 mm

Drive and electrical components

- 2 x NPC T64 24V gear motors
- 2 x 10 in wheels
- 2 x VEX BB 300A ESC (other options available)
- 2 x 300 mm servo extension leads
- 2 x OptiPower 4s 6600mA lithium polymer batteries
- 82 mm diameter x 98 mm pallet truck roller (20 mm ID bearings with plastic 12 mm reducers)
- 5 x 50A Anderson connector pairs
- 2 x EC5 connector pairs
- 1 x EC3 connector pair
- Bullet connector crimps
- 2 m red and black 10AWG flexible wire
- 2 m red and black 14AWG flexible wire
- 200A Maxi fuse and fuse holder
- Spektrum DX6e transmitter and receiver
- Dual channel RC relay
- 12V LED strip
- 100 mm cable ties
- Electrical tape
- Heatshrink in various sizes

Pneumatic components

- 100 mm bore x 250 mm stroke pneumatic cylinder, Parker P1D-B100MC-0250
- 2 x pneumatic 3/2 valves, normally closed, 24V solenoids Pneumax T772 ½in ports
- 2 kg CO_2 aluminium fire extinguisher bottle with screw-top valve (117 mm diameter)
- 2-liter stainless steel buffer tank, G 1/2 Festo air reservoir, 2-liter
- CO_2 regulator, Victor SR310b (with UK CO_2 nut)
- Legris high-pressure ball valve brass ¼ in, RS part No 231-5118
- 1 m 16 mm flexible pneumatic pipe
- 500 mm 12 mm flexible pneumatic pipe
- 500 mm 8 mm flexible pneumatic pipe
- 4 x ½ in to 16 mm straight pneumatic fittings
- 2 x ½ in to 16 mm 90° elbow pneumatic fittings
- 1 x 16 mm to 16 mm 90° elbow pneumatic fitting
- 1 x ½ in to 12 mm straight pneumatic fitting
- 1 x ½ in to 12 mm T-piece pneumatic fitting
- 1 x 12 mm to 12 mm 90° elbow pneumatic fitting
- 1 x 12 mm three-way T-piece pneumatic fitting
- 1 x ¼ in to 12 mm 90° elbow pneumatic fitting
- 1 x 12 mm male to 8 mm female reducer pneumatic fitting
- 1 x ¼ in to 8 mm 90° elbow pneumatic fitting
- PTFE tape

This build is designed to use the minimum amount of specialist tools, which may require some parts to be outsourced to engineering companies. The main parts are the Hardox chassis and axe parts, as they're very difficult to cut using traditional tools. We recommend getting them laser cut or water-jet cut. Both will give excellent results and can often be done within a couple of days cheaply. We cut these parts out on a CNC plasma cutter, as that's what we have available at Robo Challenge. Although plasma cutting doesn't give a perfect finish and tolerance, after a quick tidy up with a grinder they make perfectly good robot parts!

Hardox 3-millimeter-thick sheet components for Robot Wars challenger

3-millimeter-thick sheet with numbered parts.

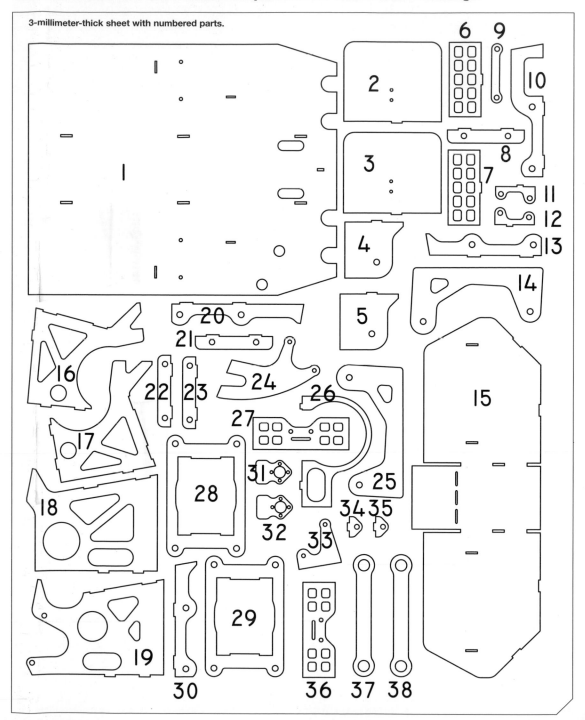

Hardox 4mm-thick sheet components for Robot Wars challenger

4-millimeter-thick sheet with lettered parts.

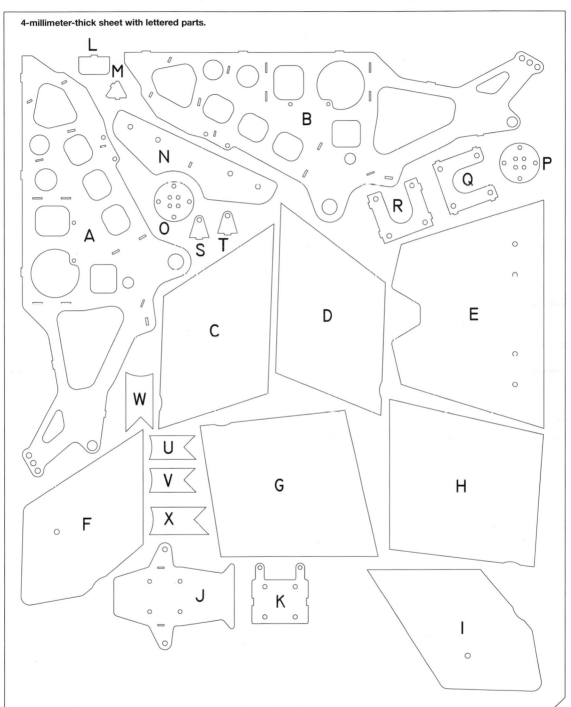

Ellis Ware – Pulsar/Magnetar

"All of our robots are built at home, in our garage. We have basic machine tools, but can't cut exotic materials like Hardox precisely enough for a project like Magnetar. In that situation, we send the CAD models to local companies with the right tools, and assemble the results at home."

The full DXF files for each sheet of Hardox are available for download at www.robotwars.tv ready to send to get cut, along with full 3D CAD models to aid in the building process. This design can either be followed exactly, as we'll be showing below, or you're free to use the CAD files provided to make your own adjustments and changes to suit your style or preferences.

From here on we'll be referring to the sheet metal parts as numbers/letters illustrated below, so marking each piece at this point will help in quickly identifying the parts required for each step.

↓ **Sparks fly on the plasma cutter.**

Main chassis build

1

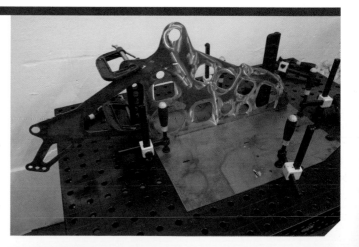

- Starting with a clean and flat workbench, take the Hardox plates "1" and "A." From this point on we recommend clamping plate "1" – which will be the main base plate for the robot – down to the bench, to avoid warping throughout assembly. The base plate is symmetrical so can be placed either way up.
- With plate "1" firmly clamped to the bench, slot bulkhead "A" into the left-hand side of the base. Note that the front of the base has half-round slots indicating its orientation.
- Using a square block or mounts, clamp the left-hand bulkhead upright, square to the base.

2

■ The mounts for the main pneumatic cylinder need to be placed in at this point, helping to tie the left and right bulkheads together.

■ Take pieces "Q" and "R," sliding them into the slots perpendicular to the front of the bulkheads. Pieces "Q" and "R" are identical and need to be mounted in the same orientation with the large U-shaped opening at the top.

3

■ Take the right-hand bulkhead "B" and slot it into the base plate as shown. Be careful to ensure that the pneumatic cylinder mounts are fully located into both the left and right bulkheads. At this point, large clamps can be used to securely hold everything solidly together.

■ The rear bump stop plate "K" can be placed into position at the rear of the bulkheads, ensuring the two protrusions are facing toward the front of the chassis.

4

■ If the bulkheads aren't vertical and square at this step of the build, then the entire chassis will become more difficult to assemble as it progresses, throwing up issues with alignment and gear mesh. If you're satisfied that they're good to go then it's time to get the welder out.

■ Though it's tempting to weld everything up solid at each stage of the build, it's very important that you initially only lightly tack-weld each stage into position sufficiently to hold it together! Tacking each part in position allows you to realign components if they aren't level. More importantly, fully welding can heavily distort sheet steel. Only once the full chassis is tacked together will we fully weld it, as by that time there'll be enough bracing and stiffness to ensure minimal deflection.

5

Extending off the side of the main bulkheads will be the main motor pods. Take part "18" and slide it into the slots on the right-hand bulkhead, level with the rear of the base plate.

Check for squareness both vertically and horizontally with a square or by eye. The tabs should keep it vertical. However, depending on the accuracy of cutting it's best to double-check before welding it in position. Tack weld in place and fit part "16" into the same side of the bulkhead and base. The slots for this are located approximately 235 millimeters from the rear plate. Again check these are square and tack-weld into position.

6

Before the build progresses too far it's worth checking the fitment of the pneumatic cylinder. If the cylinder is too tight, this is the only stage of the build where the tolerance can be altered for fitment. The cylinder should slide in nicely without too much force.

7

The end plates for the motor pods are where the motor assembly will later bolt on, so care must be taken to ensure they're correctly placed and square. Part "13" is the front end plate. Line up the tabs and clamp this piece using a square block and clamp to allow it to be tacked in position accurately.

Ensure that the tops of the two plates line up correctly (parts "13" and "20" look very similar other than in their lengths).

Once in position, repeat the same step for part "20" at the rear of the motor pod.

→ **Motor pod end plates.**

8

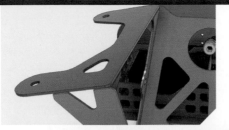

→ **Motor pod top plate. Note how the edges line up in the highlighted area.**

■ The final part of the motor pod is "14." This ties each side together and stiffens the section up. It also acts as the top armor mount later in the build.

■ Take special care to line up the back edge of this plate with the vertical motor pod end plates as shown below before welding in position.

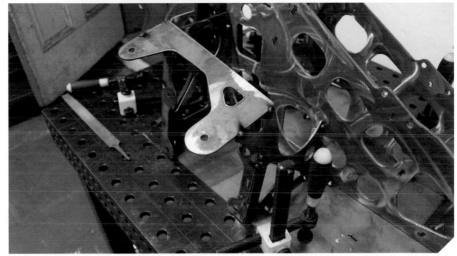

9

■ Repeat the previous steps using parts "17," "19," "10," "30" and "25" to create the other motor pod on the left-hand side of the chassis.

10

■ The next step is the main CO_2 bottle mount (part "26"). This slots into position in the bulkhead at the front left-hand side of the chassis. Tack-weld in place and check it's square to the bulkhead.

■ To stop the bottle sliding forward, repeat this step for part "L" as shown below.

→→ **CAD with bottle mount and bottle stop in position.**

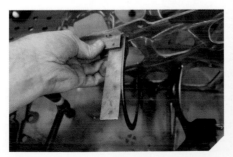

→ **Bottle mounts.**

11

■ Plate "15" will be used to make up the robot's rear base plate, where the batteries and electronics will be housed. Clamp it in a large vice, folder or workbench and fold

along the ridge to approximately 35° (fold line is illustrated below). This angle can be tweaked once in position. The rear base is symmetrical so the bend direction won't affect its position.

■ Slot the rear base into position, with the fold pointing towards the floor. The fold should line up closely with the angle of the side bulkheads. Tack-weld the rear base to the side bulkheads. Avoid welding to the drive pods until later in the build.

12

↓ **Rear panels.**

■ To stiffen up the rear base plate and protect the electronics in the back, plates "2" and "4" need to be positioned on its back edges. Using a square block, tack-weld plate "2" in position to the base and the left bulkhead. This will ensure the rear base plate is square to the rest of the machine.

■ Continue with plate "4" to stiffen up the rear of the machine. These two sections will also double as removable link mounts and rear armour mounting.

■ Repeat these steps for the right-hand side with parts "3" and "5."

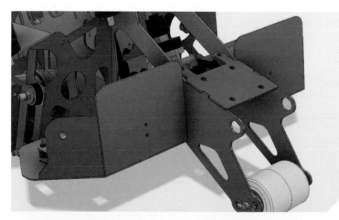

13

The final top armor mounts, "S" and "T," are now ready to be welded in position at the rear of the chassis. These need to run in line with the top of the motor pods. Slot the armor mounts into position, and with a straight edge on top of the motor pod set the angle and weld. These two pieces are identical and need to be mounted on both sides of the chassis.

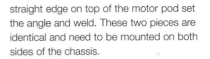

14

Take parts "34" and "35," and place them into position inside each bulkhead as shown below. These must be square and welded in position. They're the mounts for the rear valve cover. The cover needs to sit flat on top, so care must be taken to weld underneath only.

15

The battery box is next to be assembled, going in the rear right-hand side of the chassis. This box is purposefully large to accommodate a wide range of batteries whilst also allowing space for hard foam mounting.

Take parts "6" and "7," and, using a square or block, slot them into the rear base plate as shown below. Tack-weld in place. Parts "27" and "36" can now be placed into position and welded. Notice the slots in the center of parts "27" and "36." These will later be used for large straps to hold the batteries in place. TERRORHURTZ uses this same method with excellent results.

16

■ Next up is mounting the main solenoid valves for firing the weapon. For this step you'll need two 16 mm to ½ in BSP straight pneumatic fittings, one of the valves and part "24."

■ Loosely screw one of the fittings into the base of the pneumatic cylinder by hand, and the other into port 2 of the solenoid valve. These only need to be finger-tight for now, since initially they'll only be used for visual alignment.

■ The valve can be bolted to part "24" ensuring the orientation is correct as laid out below.

■ Line up the two pneumatic fittings both vertically and horizontally before tack-welding the mount in position to the right-hand bulkhead. Once it's held in position, remove the valve from the mounting bracket.

17

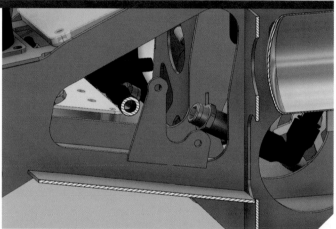

■ Piece "33," the rear valve mount, must be mounted in the rear right-hand side near the battery box. For this part, don't bolt the valve in position whilst tacking as the heat may damage the plastic casing.

■ The valve mount must be mounted approximately 35 to 40 millimeters from the motor pod and between 18 to 20 millimeters high, parallel to the rear base plate as shown in the 3D model on the right. A test-fit of the valve at this stage may be useful to ensure that the fittings are clear of any obstructions.

→ **Rear valve mount.**

18

➜➜ **Dump position.**

■ Mounting the dump valve in any robot requires careful thought to ensure that it can be easily accessed very close to the main CO_2 bottle valve and the removable link. On this robot it's located on the left bulkhead at the back.

■ Remove the handle from the valve and bolt it into the mount temporarily, and put the handle back in place. The dump valve mount must be placed so that with the handle vertical and in line with the top port of the valve there's between 5 and 10 millimeters of clearance minimum, as shown in the 3D model.

■ Tack the bracket in place and remove the valve before welding securely.

■ Part "M," the front armor mount support, is to be located at the very front of the robot, between the bulkheads. Slot into position and tack-weld square to the base plate.

■ The chassis can now by unclamped from the workbench. It should be very solid and secure at this point. Raise the front of the chassis up approximately 6 millimeters off the bench with a bar or spacer, and place the front armor mount "N" on the front of the machine, slotting into the front armor mount support. Make sure this is perfectly level with the workbench and the base of the robot. If the front armor mount isn't welded on level, this will be exaggerated by the main armor when mounted. This should be tack-welded to the base plate and the two bulkheads.

➜ **Front armor mount brace.**

➜➜ **Front armor mount.**

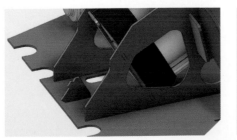

■ The main chassis is now complete and ready
for welding. All the joints and parts should be
welded at this stage, including underneath
the chassis and the tab/slot joins.

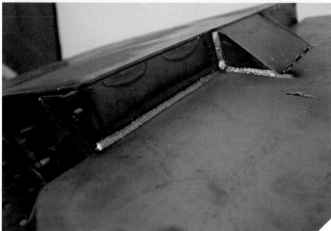

Sam Smith –
Carbide lead
designer/engineer

❝ High-strength wear-plate steels
like Hardox or Raex are ideal for
creating a monocoque chassis. When
welding up a chassis of this type, it's
best to try and minimize the amount of
heat input, as this weakens the parent
metal. This can be achieved by keeping
weld runs short and allowing the part
time to cool slightly between runs. As
with traditional sheet fabrications, it's
often a good idea to tack the chassis
together or keep it held in place using
a jig to avoid distortion, and build up
the weld stitches gradually
and evenly around the chassis to
minimize distortion to the structure. ❞

■ In this step we'll be making the front bump stop assembly. This holds the large rubber stop, limiting the axe from overshooting and hitting a solid end stop inside the cylinder. It also doubles up as protection for the very thin-walled aluminium cylinder. TERRORHURTZ suffered from a lack of protection, leading to Shunt putting a hole right in the middle of it during Rogue House Robot in Series 9!

■ Taking the main protection plate, part "J," fold the two side protrusions slightly down. This can be done in a folder or with a vice and large lump hammer.

■ Parts "11" and "12" slot into the underside of the main protection plate, square and parallel to each other, and welded on the outside edges. Note that the orientation of the mounts must be correct and the welds MUST be on the outside edges or the plate won't fit on to the chassis.

■ Finally, mount the rubber bump stop using four short M8 bolts and lock nuts.

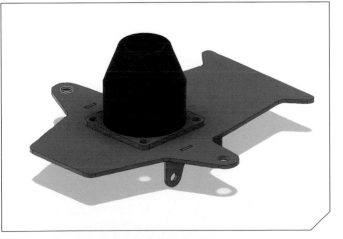

→ **Front bump stop assembly.**

- The motor mounts comprise of three parts – "8," "22" and "28." Although very similar, "8" and "22" are different, so double-check you have the correct components at this point.
- Clamp motor bracket "8" square along the inside edge of main mount "28," and tack in position. Repeat this for motor bracket "22" on the opposite side. Weld the outer joins, being careful to leave a minimum of 15 mm clearance from the bolt holes. Flip the motor mount over and weld the taps on the back for maximum strength, again being careful not to weld the inside of the motor brackets.
- Repeat this for parts "21," "23" and "29."

↑ **Note the different hole positions between the parts.**

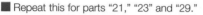

- Slide the brackets over the back of the NPC motors as shown below and bolt in position using four 5/16-24 UNF bolts per motor.

- Check that the Oilite bushes fit comfortably into the bulkheads, pressing them in from the inside edge of each bulkhead.
- If they're too tight, use a round file to clean up the holes in the bulkhead until the bushes are a nice tap fit into the holes.

→ **Pneumatic cylinder is only in place for test fitting.**

25

- On both wheels, remove the four bolts holding the hub and bearing assembly to the rims.
- Once removed, use this opportunity to remove the rims completely and add some glue to stop the tyres from slipping in

combat. Bolt plates "O" and "P" to the rims through the four holes, using the nuts and bolts removed from the hubs.
- Keep the wheels to one side until later in the assembly process.

26

- The pneumatic cylinder comes as standard with a smooth round piston rod. These next steps explain how to replace the piston rod with 2.5 Mod round rack that will mesh perfectly with the main gear on the axe.
- Remove the four bolts in the top cap of the cylinder and slide out the piston rod and piston.

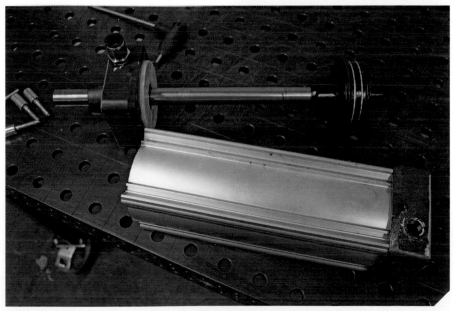

■ Clamp the piston rod in a vice or lathe and remove the bolt in the base of the piston using an Allen key. The bolts can often be covered in Loctite and be very difficult to remove, requiring a longer bar on the end of the Allen key.

■ There are two ways to modify the rack to fit the piston. We'll run through the simpler option here, and supply a drawing for the more robust but complicated method at the end of this section. Mount the 2.5 Mod round rack in a lathe and drill an 8.5 millimeter diameter hole approximately 40 millimeters deep. Tap in a thread the full depth using an M10 tap.

■ Reassemble the piston on to the round rack with an M10 bolt and washer. Use Loctite on the bolt at this point so that you don't need to strip everything down again if it comes loose.

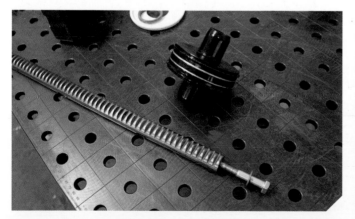

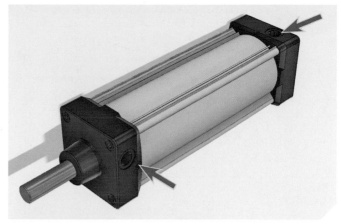

Insert the piston back into the cylinder. Be careful to push the seal in evenly all the way around. Any pinches in the seal could lead to the piston leaking past it or the seal tearing after use. When assembling the top cap back on to the cylinder, rotate it 90° clockwise so that when the port on the lower end cap is facing upwards the port in the top end cap is facing to the right as illustrated. Tighten all four bolts and ensure the piston rod is moving up and down smoothly.

The final modification to the rack is to cut it to length. Push the piston rod all the way down and cut off at approximately 70 millimeters from the very end of the end cap.

Mount ram in chassis.

The cylinder can now be bolted into the chassis with eight M10 bolts (four in the top cap and four in the lower end cap). Ensure the top port is facing down towards the base of the robot and the lower port is facing to the right.

↑ **The ram endcaps should be positioned with the ports as shown (arrows).**

27

- Making the shafts is fairly straightforward for this robot. We've removed the need to tap a thread and other more complex methods by holding our shafts in place using split pins. Split pins are great for this sort of thing as long as they're not subject to extremely high loads, as they allow the shafts to be quickly removed for repairs. The drawing gives all the measurements needed.
- Cut the 25-mm ground steel bars, 12-mm ground steel bar and the 30-mm tube using either a hacksaw in a vice or ideally a chop saw, to get clean and square cuts.
- Clean the cut edges with a sander, adding a small chamfer to help with locating the shafts during assembly.

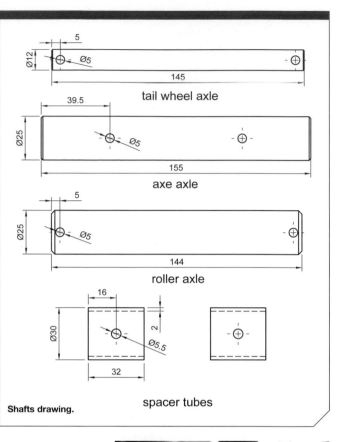

tail wheel axle

axe axle

roller axle

spacer tubes

Shafts drawing.

- Using a 5-mm drill bit, drill the holes in each of the shafts as shown in the drawing and de-burr to provide a smooth outer finish.

28

- Mount the rear bump stop on the back of the chassis using the four M8 lock nuts and bolts.

→ **Rear bump stop.**

29

■ To make the axe assembly you'll need parts "U," "V," "W," "X," the main axe arm, the remaining two 10-mm-thick plates and the 52T 2.5 MOD gear.

■ Placing the axe arm and gear together on a flat surface, stack up parts "U," "W" and one of the 10-mm plates as shown below, using a 25-mm bar to align the pivot holes.

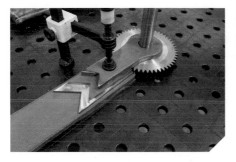

■ Ensure that the pivot hole is central to the axe shaft and the gear is butted up against the end of the axe then tack-weld each layer into position. DO NOT weld the gear in position at this point.

■ Flip the axe over and repeat with parts "V," "X" and the remaining 10-mm plate.

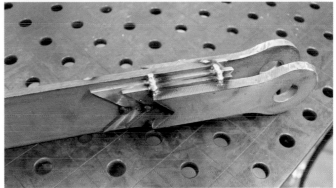

30

■ With ram in position and the gear teeth facing up, assemble axe and gear into position with the shaft, ensuring the axe arm is resting on the rear bump stop.

- Push the piston rod fully in and mark its position with a marker. Pull the piston rod out 10 millimeters and tack-weld the gear to the axe assembly on both sides. It's a useful sanity check at this point to manually swing the axe over and make sure that it rotates until the axe head is below the base of the chassis.

- The axe can now be removed from the chassis and welded up fully. This needs to be a strong weld to ensure it withstands the shocks and forces to which it'll be subjected. Be careful not to weld the teeth directly, and clean off any weld spatter that could lock up the gears. The axe assembly is now complete.

31

- Take the roller axle (the shorter of the 25-millimeter bars made earlier) and the 25-millimeter ID grooved bearing. Assemble the rear roller as shown in the image on the right. You may need to loosen the pneumatic cylinder mounting bolts to make assembly easier, ensuring that there's no gap between the piston rod and the grooved bearing when tightening it up. Secure the shaft in place with 4-millimeter split pins on either side.

➔ **Rear roller.**

32

■ The axe assembly can now be mounted using the axe axle (longer 25-millimeter bar made earlier) and the two spacer tubes made earlier.

■ Again, pull the piston rod out 10 millimeters from its fully retracted position and place the axe in the robot, ensuring the arm is on the rear bump stop. Slide the axe axle through the Oilite bushes, using the two spacer tubes either side of the axe. Finish the assembly by pinning with four 4-millimeter split pins. Again, double-check that the axe rotates fully over the top of the robot.

→ **Axe assembly.**

33

■ Mount the 40-millimeter x 15-millimeter rubber mounts to the motor pods using M10 lock nuts. The motors can now be mounted to the chassis. With the motor body towards the front of the chassis and the shaft towards the back, slide the motor mount on to the rubber mounts and fasten with M10 lock nuts and washers.

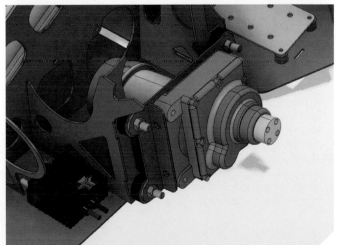

→ **Motor mounting.**

34

■ The front bump stop assembly can also be mounted at this point. Using four M8 bolts and nuts, line the mounting holes up with the holes in the bulkheads above the pneumatic cylinder and bolt in position.

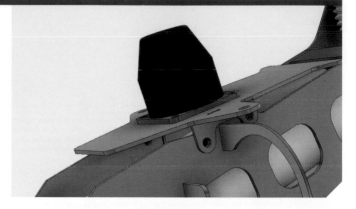

→ **Front bump stop mounting.**

35

■ Using the 12-mm tail wheel axle made earlier, mount the tail wheel to the tail of the robot in the central of the three holes. These positions can be altered depending on wheel size, wear or ground clearance required. Space the wheel with M12 washers either side before securing in position with 4-mm split pins. The robot's tail is critical with an axe, and helps minimize the lift the front of the robot gets when the axe is fired. The longer the tail the better!

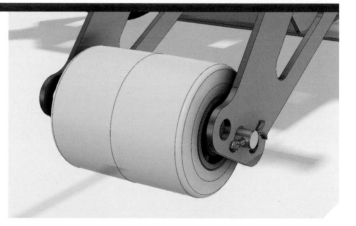

→ **Tail wheel assembly.**

36

■ The buffer tank stores the regulated CO_2 at around 8–12 bar for this robot. Although, being stainless steel, it can physically be welded to the chassis, it's certainly not recommended. Not only will this void its pressure certification and fail safety checks, but if the welds aren't done correctly vibration could cause fracture points on the tank.

■ To mount the tank, place on the right-hand side of the chassis, lining up the two holes. Secure using M6 lock nuts and bolts.

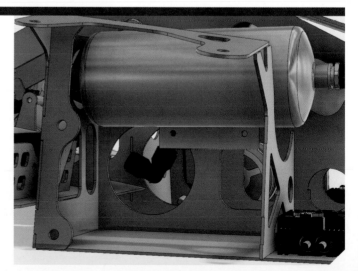

→ **Buffer mod.**

37

At this point we're going to start adding the pneumatic fittings and joining all the segments of the pneumatic system together.

The pneumatic fittings normally come with a small amount of thread seal on them when new. However, we recommend always using PTFE tape wrapped around the threads before tightening them up to avoid unexpected gas leaks.

Screw the ½-in to 16-mm elbow fitting into the front port on the buffer tank, and a ½-in to 12-mm straight fitting into the rear port. The flow rate of the gas is critical to making an effective pneumatic axe, which is why we're using the largest pipes and fittings directly from the buffer tank to the cylinder whilst minimizing the distance and the number of fittings in between. We can use smaller pipe and fittings from the regulator to the buffer tank as this is a much lower flow rate area, and the retract valve also doesn't need to be as effective as the main valve.

Screw ½-in to 16-mm straight fittings into the lower end cap in the pneumatic cylinder and output port 2 on the front valve. Input port 1 on the same valve requires a ½-in to 16-mm 90° elbow fitting. Once these are tightly in position use a pneumatic pipe cutter to cut a short length of 16-mm pipe to join the valve to the cylinder. When the pipe is the correct length and the holes to the valve line up with its mount, bolt the valve in position. Large pneumatic fittings often require a lot of force to push together, so make sure the pipe is fully pushed in before removing to trim. To save time and waste, when cutting pneumatic piping you should cut the pipe longer than you need, try it and then trim it down until it's the correct length.

Cut another length of 16-mm pipe to join the valve to the buffer tank's 16-mm fitting. Having flexible pipe helps here where a bend is required. If your pipe is too stiff to curve 90° without kinking, a 90° 16-mm to 16-mm elbow would be required.

↑ Buffer fittings.

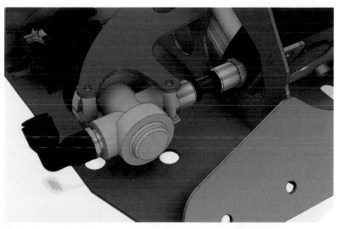
↑ Front ram valve fittings.

■ The firing side of the pneumatic circuit is now complete. Moving to the rear of the machine, use a ½-in to 16-mm straight fitting screw into the pneumatic cylinder's top cap port facing downwards. Another of these fittings is to be screwed into outlet port 2 on the rear retract valve. Whilst the valve is out of the robot, screw the ½-in to 12-mm T-piece fitting into inlet port 1.

■ At this point the valve can be bolted into place using two M5 nuts and bolts.

■ The angle between the valve and cylinder is too tight to curve the pipe, so using a 16mm to 16-mm 90° elbow cut two sections of 16-mm pipe and fit between the valve and cylinder.

■ Similarly to above, using a 12-mm to 12-mm 90° elbow cut two pieces of 12-mm pipe and join the valve to the buffer tank.

■ Cut a short section of 12-mm pipe and insert it into the other side of the T-piece on the valve. This piece wants to be as short as possible, but be careful to make sure that it's fully pushed all the way in to ensure it fits properly with the next fitting.

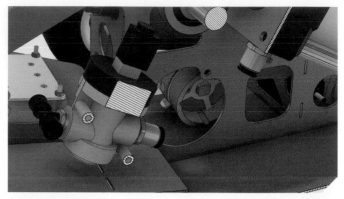
↑ **Rear ram and valve fittings.**

↓ **T-piece pipe.**

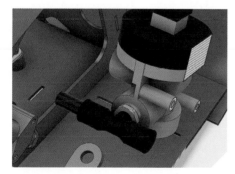

■ Screw the ¼-in to 8-mm 90° elbow into the top of the dump valve. Then, using the 12-mm T-piece and 12-mm to 8-mm reducer, assemble together as shown below. Cut a length of 8-mm pipe to join the dump valve to the 8-mm reducer. This puts the dump valve directly in line with the regulator and buffer tank with no obstructions, allowing for fast and safe venting of gas at the end of a battle.

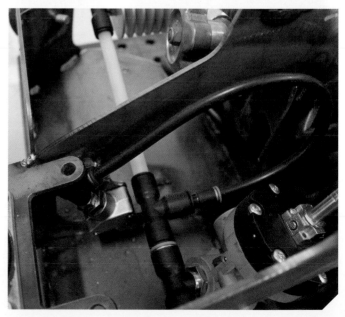

■ Screw in the final fitting, a ¼-in to 12-mm 90° elbow into the output on the regulator, and attach to the rest of the system using a length of 12-mm tube. Slot the main CO_2 bottle into position on the left-hand side and bolt the bottle clamp (part "9") to the motor pod. The pneumatic system should now be complete.

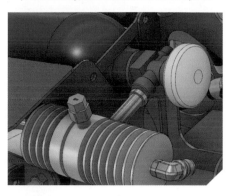

← **Bottle clamp.**

38

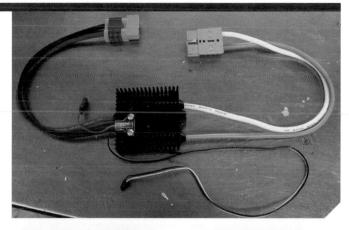

■ Begin the wiring by soldering the Anderson connectors on to the drive ESCs. We're using VEX BB 300A speed controllers for this build. They're certainly not the cheapest option available for the power we require, but they've been proven to be very reliable by robots such as Carbide and Apollo. More cost-effective options such as the RageBridge 2 can be used as a replacement and have been proven to work in the arena with these same motors.

■ Check carefully the polarity of the connectors, as plugging power to the ESCs backwards will immediately destroy them. As the same connector type is being used for input and output, mark the input connector to make it clearly identifiable.

■ The programming cable and RX cables should be plugged into the ESC at this point too. Leave the short programming cable in place permanently, as this will be useful for future programming if required.

■ Mount the ESCs to the base of the chassis as shown, one either side of the robot next to the drive pods.

→ **VEX BB mounting.**

39

■ The same connectors can now be soldered to the drive motors and plugged into the ESCs. Put a cable tie around any connectors like these that don't need disconnecting between fights.

40

■ The wiring diagram shows the complete circuit required to make the robot work.
■ For ease of maintenance and wiring we've split the wiring loom into three parts: the main wiring loom, the RC relay wiring and the solenoid wiring.
■ The first to make up is the main wiring loom. Following the diagram, run the cables through the chassis from component to component to measure the lengths required. Always add a bit extra to ensure that cables aren't tight or rubbing on sharp edges.
■ Be careful to ensure the correct polarity on all the connectors, and dry-fit them before applying power to double-check.
■ Starting at the batteries, solder the EC5 connectors in series, with the main +ve cable going directly to the removable link (to be located on the left side of the robot). From

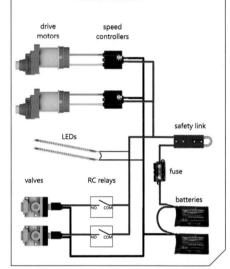

ROBOT WIRING

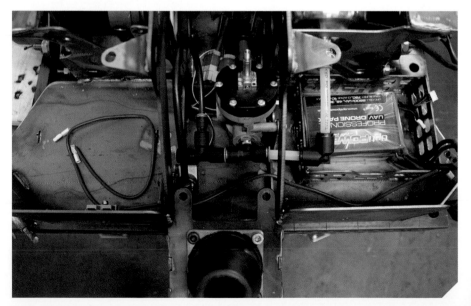

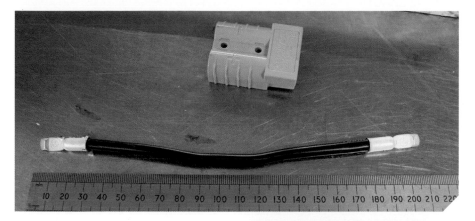

the link, three +ve cables need to run power to each of the drive ESCs, and another to the RC relays to power the solenoid valves.

■ The 0V cable from the batteries needs to go directly to the drive ESCs. To keep the number of wires to a minimum, the 0V supply to the solenoids can be tapped directly from the drive ESC connector.

■ The removable link is very simple to make. Taking a short length of wire, solder up the connectors to make a loop from one side of the connector to the other. Ensure your wire is long enough that you can easily put two or three fingers through to pull the link out.

■ The main wiring loom is almost complete, only requiring the addition of bullet connectors to link the wiring loom to the RC switcher and solenoids, and a supply to the power light.

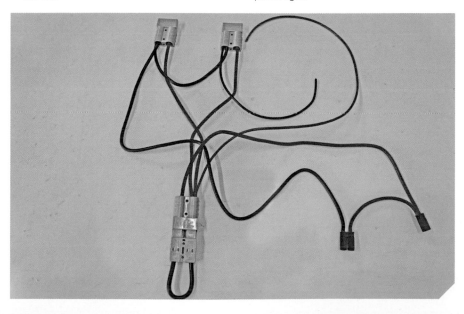

41

■ The RC relay can now be wired up. This has a single plug to the receiver using only one channel. However, it uses two relays to control both of the valves in our robot. When the weapon stick is up it'll activate one relay, and when it's down it will activate the other.

■ Wire a single power wire into the common on the first relay, with a jumper cable over to the common on the second relay. Crimp a male bullet connector on to the input of the power wire.

■ Because we don't want either of the valves powered up until we activate them, wire the two output cables to each of the normally open connectors. To make it easier to attach to the solenoids, solder an EC3 to the output wires. Polarity in this instance doesn't matter as they're both +ve.

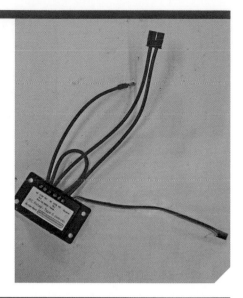

42

■ Remove the solenoids from the top of each valve and measure the cable length required to reach between the two. Solder an EC3 to the end of two long red wires. The wire from each side of the EC3 connector must go to each solenoid separately to be able to trigger them individually with a +ve voltage.

■ Using black wire, make a short length with a crimped male bullet connector and solder to one of the solenoids. Again using black wire,

solder a jumper cable from one solenoid directly to the next. This is the permanent 0V to the solenoid valves directly to the main wiring loom. At this point, to reduce noise and interference it's recommended to solder a diode across the terminals of each solenoid (note the polarity of the diode). Always cover any open solder joints with heat shrink.

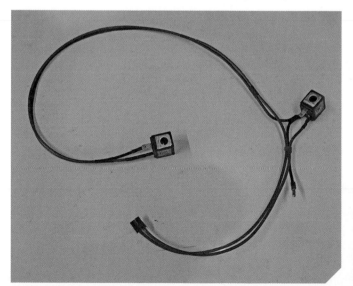

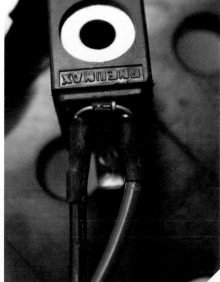

■ Adding the power leads to the LEDs is simple in this circuit. Cut two more lengths of red and black low-power cable and crimp to the existing loose cables in the main wiring loom using female bullet connectors. These bullet connectors will be the supply to the RC switcher and the solenoids. The LED output can have either an EC3 or another convenient low-power connector attached.

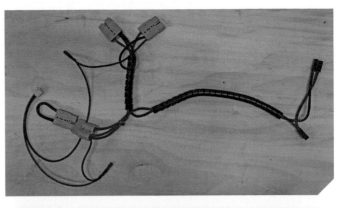

■ Finally, tidy up the wiring loom with cable ties and sheathing to avoid it rubbing on sharp edges of the chassis.

■ Bolt the link on to the rear left panel in the chassis and route the wiring through the chassis to the correct locations.

■ The next major safety component required in all robots running lithium polymer batteries is a fuse. The fuse must be mounted directly after the battery connections to minimize any cabling in between. The fuse is there to protect the batteries in case of an electrical short in the robot, and must be rated below the maximum discharge of the battery. In this case we're installing a 200A mega fuse.

■ Bolt the fuse holder into position and split the wiring loom cable to suit. Solder 8-mm ring terminals to the wire you've just split and bolt to each side of the fuse. Add the top cover back on to make sure there are no bare electrical connections.

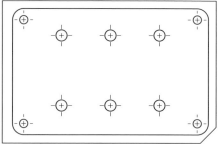

- Most LED strips available are 12V as standard. To avoid wiring in resistors, wire two short LED strips in series. Again, make sure all electrical connections are covered with heat shrink or tape. Then connect the LED strips to the LED power cables on the main wiring loom and mount inside the bulkheads where they'll be clearly visible.
- The more delicate electronics, such as the receiver and RC relays, are best rubber mounted to help minimise shock and vibration during battles.
- Make a mount by printing out the PDF templates available online at www.robotwars.tv We made the mount using aluminium, but any metal or flexible plastic should work well. Lightly glue the printed layout to the sheet of aluminium and cut around with a saw.

↑ **Radio tray drawing.**

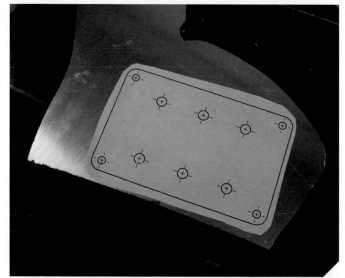

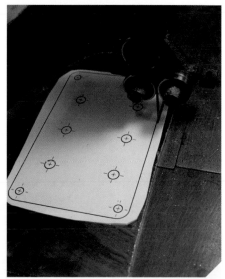

- Once the profile has been cut out, remove any sharp edges will a file before progressing.
- Using the printed-out template as a guide, center-punch the holes and drill and countersink to avoid sharp edges. Remove the paper template and clean the aluminium ready for assembly.

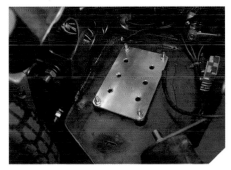

- Bolt the four small rubber mounts in position in the left-hand side of the chassis, slide the electronics plate on top and bolt in. The receiver and RC relays can now be mounted using strong double-sided tape and secured with a cable tie through the aluminium plate. It's good practice to secure the cables to stop them vibrating and moving as a result of shocks, causing breaks or issues where they join the electronics.
- At this point the ESCs and RC relay can be plugged into the receiver. Location of the receiver leads entirely depends on the user's preference. However, we connected the drive ESCs to Aileron and Elevator channels, and the RC relay for the weapon to the Throttle channel.

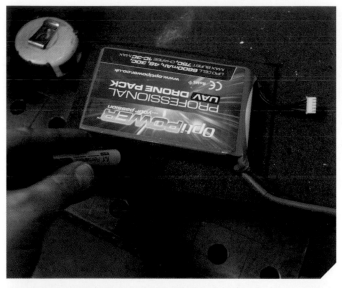

← **OptiPower 4s 6600mA lithium polymer battery.**

■ The battery tray is designed larger than the batteries not just to allow a wider range of packs but also to allow space for foam around the batteries to avoid damage during a battle.

■ Using stiff packing foam, cut a rectangle the size of the battery box and use a battery to draw around in order to cut out the internal shape. The foam can be cut with a sharp knife or saw. Using double-sided tape, stick the foam to the base of the chassis in the battery box and place the two lithium polymer batteries inside. Secure the batteries with a strap utilizing the slots in the battery box.

■ The solenoids must be screwed back on to the valves, connecting the +ve and 0V wires to the RC relay and main wiring loom respectively to complete the wiring.

■ The VEX BB controllers don't come out of the box with the BEC (battery eliminator circuit) active. Using the short programming lead on the ESC, activate the BEC using a laptop. Instructions on how to do this will be included with the ESC or online. The BEC is a 5V low power supply that powers the receiver. DO NOT activate the BEC on both ESCs as this may cause issues when in use.

■ Without gas pressure or attaching the wheels, plug the link in and test the function of the robot.

43

With the electronics tested, mount the wheels to the motor gearbox using four 5/16-24 UNF bolts on each wheel.

44

■ Bolt the six 60-mm diameter rubber mounts to the chassis as shown, using M10 lock nuts. The rubber mounts will support the armor and help to reduce shock throughout the robot in combat.

■ The main body armor is completely independent from the rest of the chassis,

allowing it to be removed by undoing only six bolts for easy access to everything internally. 4-mm Hardox is being used in this machine, which is more than enough for live events and shows and will even stand up well on *Robot Wars*. There's spare weight to increase this thickness if required.

↓ **Armor rubber mounts.**

↘ **Armor assembly v1.**

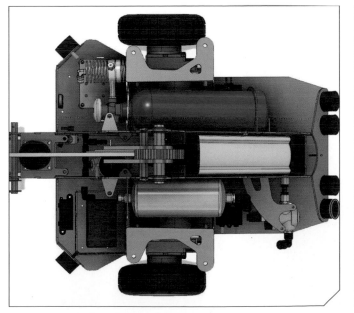

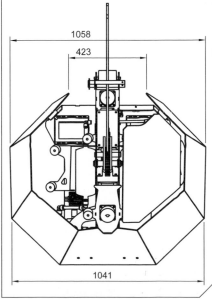

1058
423
1041

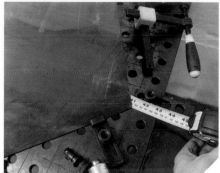

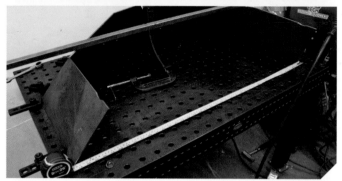

■ Using armor plates "E," "G" and "H," align the edges and tack-weld roughly in position. Measure the distance between the back of the two plates and clamp into position.

■ At this point it can be useful to tack-weld a bar across the top of the armor to keep it rigid in position whilst lining up and tack-welding pieces "C" and "D." Again, measure the width and tack-weld another bar along the top to hold securely.

■ The final parts, "I" and "F," can now be lined up and tacked in position. Cut a 423-mm-wide length of bar and tack-weld it between the two rear panels to accurately set the width. The armor can now be welded up solid all the way around, and once cooled the positioning bars can be removed.

↓ **Clean, good-quality welding.**

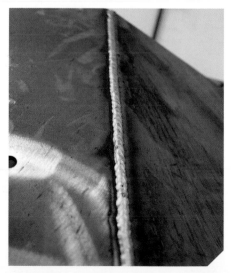

45

■ We're using 10-mm polycarbonate for the top protection of this robot. Polycarbonate is an excellent material to use to deflect axe hits and other impacts due to its flexible and shock-absorbing properties. However, polycarbonate can crack if it's bolted down too tight or to solid mounts. You should therefore use large rubber mounts to secure the polycarbonate to the chassis, allowing it to flex and bend under impacts.

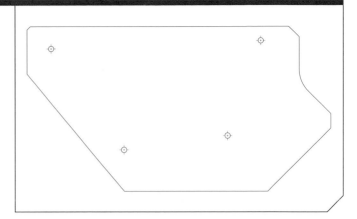

→ **Top armor pattern.**

■ Print out two copies of the "Top Armour Pattern" available online at www.robotwars.tv. These PDFs can be printed full size over six A4 sheets each. Line up the pattern and tape the printouts together to make two large templates. One will be used for the left side, and one for the right. Using thin double-sided tape, stick the templates to the polycarbonate sheet.
■ Cut around the armor template using a jigsaw and finish off by drilling the 10.5-mm mounting holes. Clean up the edges with a file and the top armor panels are ready to fit.

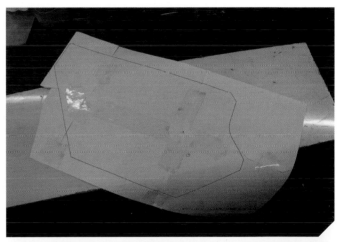

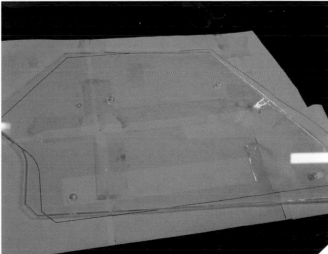

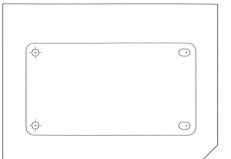

↑ **Cover rear drawing.**

■ Mount the four 50-mm diameter rubber mounts on each side of the chassis and bolt the top armor panels directly to these using M10 x 15 bolts.

■ Repeat the same process above for the "Cover Rear Drawing" and mount to the back of the chassis above the rear valve, using four M6 x 20-mm bolts and lock nuts.

■ The final part to make is a critical safety feature – the locking bar. All fast-moving active weapons require a locking bar, but they're often an afterthought.

■ Using parts "37" and "38" and two lengths of 20-mm diameter tube 195 mm long, slot together, clamp and weld as shown, using a spacer block of approximately 25 mm between parts "37" and "38."

The only thing left to do is to paint your robot to suit your preferences. Then your *Robot Wars* Challenger is complete and ready for battle!

↓ **Locking bar.**

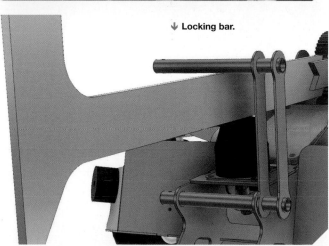

← Finished robot.

Warning

Robots are extremely dangerous, and extreme care must be taken with them at all times. We recommend attending live events to meet the teams and see their robots close up before using a robot like the challenger. Before attempting to test it yourself, take your finished robot to an event and test it in the safety of an arena, with experienced teams around who can help you.

7
How to win
Robot Wars

Now that you've built your robot and understand how the competition works and the judging criteria, how do you win *Robot Wars*? When it comes to winning, *Robot Wars* has no specific solution. This is indeed the reason why teams love taking part and finding their own compelling solutions to take the trophy. The reality that you can't spend your way to the top or design the perfect robot means that creativity can flourish. There's no guaranteed way to win.

However, having said that, there are some very good tips on how to perform to your team's full potential – how to prepare in order to give your team its best chance. It comes down to preparation, design and strategy. Michael Oates gives us a really helpful insight into how to compete successfully in *Robot Wars*: "The most important thing to remember is that

Robot Wars is a long competition, and you've got to fight your way through a lot of battles if you want to reach the Grand Final. Survivability is what gives a finalist or champion the edge over robots eliminated early on – even if you bring the ultimate fighting robot into Round 1, if it can't keep performing a few fights later then it's never going to make it all the way. This means preparation before the competition and the reliability of your robot are absolutely crucial. But survivability also depends massively upon your strategies in the arena.

"With that in mind, your default strategy in the arena should always be offense. The best way to survive through the competition is to win your fights by knockouts, and as quickly as possible, since this reduces the amount of time available for your opponent to inflict damage. Battles in *Robot Wars* are only three minutes

⬇ Michael and father Adrian prepare Eruption for battle.

↑ A rather battle-weary Eruption!

long, so you have to be aggressive and take control of the fight immediately. Otherwise it can be quite hard to recover in the available time limit – and that's if you haven't been wrecked within the first minute!

"That's not to say all-out aggression is always the smartest tactic. This is more often the case in group battles, or huge melees. Generally most drivers find they're only able to properly focus on one opponent at once, so here being too aggressive can often be risky due to exposing weaker areas of your robot to other opponents you aren't focusing on. Sometimes there may be other factors to consider, such as there being more than one winner or not having a time limit, both of which can make a defensive approach more valid. However, except in the rarest of circumstances, you'll still have to attack your opponents to win the fight, which makes it really important to get the balance right between offense and defense.

This is why roboteers generally much prefer head-to-head fights. They're much easier to prepare strategies for!

"Your tactics will always largely depend upon your individual robot. As someone who usually drives flippers, I have to focus on out-maneuvering my opponents to get underneath them and position them towards a lower arena side wall, whereas drivers of spinners often have to focus on not engaging their opponent for a certain amount of time in order to get their weapon up to maximum speed. You also have to think carefully about your opponent. For example, if you're fighting a robot with particularly powerful drive, letting the Pit open is probably not a good idea! The opponents you have to think most carefully about are spinners, which are so destructive that not only might they cause you to lose a fight, they might also cause you damage that'll hinder you for the rest of the competition. Whilst fighting spinners

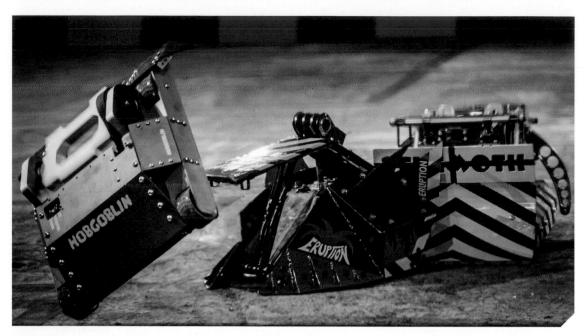

↑ Eruption gets a flip on Hobgoblin during a group battle.

↓ Eruption ganged up on by Behemoth and Cobra.

you have to consider firstly how you could avoid getting hit by their weapon, and secondly, if this isn't possible, how to make sure you only get hit on the strongest part of your robot.

"One thing everyone has to consider for all of their fights is the arena itself. A lot of the arena hazards may not be particularly destructive in themselves (most of the top robots won't be taking much damage from the Floor Flipper or Spikes), but their biggest impact is in disrupting your strategy and allowing your opponent to take control. Driving over an arena hazard is never a good thing, so my best piece of advice is to keep

← *Robot Wars* Christmas special – Matilda on the prowl.

↓ The goal for all the roboteers – the *Robot Wars* trophy.

away from them. That said, you can also use them to your own advantage against your opponents. The Floor Flipper and Spikes can allow you to get underneath or position yourself towards a more vulnerable area of your opponent, while the Pit can be used for an instant knockout win.

"The biggest arena hazards, of course, are the House Robots, which are definitely destructive in themselves and always best kept away from. Delivering your opponent to Matilda's flywheel or Shunt's axe can be a deciding factor in any fight, especially if your robot is designed more around control than to be destructive itself. You also never know which House Robots will be in the arena with you until just before each fight, which always keeps you on your toes in terms of tactics!

"The final and most important piece of advice is to think everything through carefully, and then try and remain calm before and during your fights. Driving skill and tactics are just as important as your robot's own abilities in the arena, so while hearing 'Roboteers, stand by' can be incredibly nerve-racking before a battle, try your best to stay composed. Your time in the arena is your chance to show everyone what your team and your robot can do, so give it everything you've got, and good luck!"

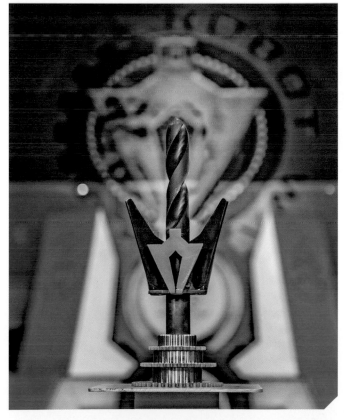

8

Appendices

The rules competitors have to follow

Every robot that you see competing in *Robot Wars* has been developed to a very high standard and adheres to the official *Robot Wars* build rules. Following these rules not only ensures a fair competition but also a safe one.

The rules contain all the information you need to build a compliant robot and cover everything you need to know, from power to weight and weapons to drive. We've included an overview of the latest set of build rules for you to follow (correct at the time of writing) and picked out some of the key areas to which you should pay close attention when designing and building your robot. We also recommend that you visit the official *Robot Wars* website (www.robotwars.tv) and download your own set of build rules to ensure you have the full and latest version.

A – Build rules

Note: The build rules evolve from series to series, and the rules quoted here are those that applied to Series 9 and 10.

1. General

1.1 Participation – All participants build and operate robots at their own risk. *Robot Wars* is inherently dangerous.

1.2 Event rules – Compliance with all event rules is mandatory. It is expected that competitors stay within the rules and procedures of their own accord and do not require constant policing.

1.3 Safety inspections – *Robot Wars* will be operating safety and rule compliance checks prior to any robot competing or testing during the event [Tech checks]. It is at the inspector's sole discretion that your robot is allowed to compete. As a builder you are obligated to disclose all operating principles and potential dangers to the inspection staff.

1.4 Cardinal safety rules – Failure to comply with any of the cardinal safety rules set out below by *Robot Wars* may result in expulsion from the event or, worse, injury and death.

1.5.1 Activation – Proper activation and deactivation of robots is critical. Robots should only be activated in the arena or testing areas with expressed consent of *Robot Wars* and its safety officials. All activation and de-activation of robots must be completed from outside the arena barrier or within specially designated areas.

1.5.2 Weapon restraints – All robots not in an arena or official testing area should have secure safety covers over any sharp edges and restraints on any active weapons or pinch hazards.

1.5.3 Carrying cradles – All robots not in an arena or official testing area should be raised on their carrying cradles in a manner so that their motive power cannot cause movement if the robot were turned on, or cannot roll or fall off the pit tables.

1.5.4 Restrictions – In some situations the safety inspection team may deem it necessary to place restrictions on your robot's operation for safety purposes. It is entirely your responsibility that these restrictions are adhered to at all times.

1.5.5 Power tools – It is expected that builders will follow all basic safety practices such as gloves and goggles when operating any machinery. The use of welders, grinders and other equipment that may produce smoke, debris or other harmful substances is not permitted in the pits area and is only permitted in dedicated workshop areas.

2. Weight classification

2.1 Weight limit – The maximum weight limit allowed for the Heavyweight category is 110 kg. The maximum weight limit allowed for the Featherweight category is 13.6 kg other than for "Legged robots" and "Shufflers" where the weight limits are as set out in Clause 2.2.

2.2 Legged robots – Legged robots (Walkers) may have an extra 35 kg weight allowance bringing the total to 145 kg for Heavyweight robots. Featherweight robots may have an extra 4 kg bringing the total to 17.6 kg. A Walker must employ moveable legs to support its weight. Each leg must have at least 2° of freedom. Robots with rolling or sliding mechanisms (Shufflers) will be given a 15 kg weight allowance bringing the total to 125 kg in the Heavyweight category and an extra 1.5 kg for Featherweight robots bringing the total to 15.1 kg. For clarification please disclose as much information (as possible) about your robot's drive mechanism during the application stage.

2.3 Consumables – Maximum weight includes all consumables such as CO_2 gas.

2.4 Safety equipment – Maximum weight does not include safety bars, straps, or similar equipment used to immobilize moving arms or weapons and that are removed during competition.

2.5 Active weapons – All robots must incorporate an active offensive weapon which is designed to damage, immobilize or seriously affect the operation of the opponent's robot. Weapon specifications must be included on your application form for approval. No additional or major changes to weaponry will be allowed during the event.

2.6 Interchangeable weapons – If interchangeable weapons are used, the weight is measured with the heaviest set-up in place. Please see rule 12.11 for interchangeable weapon and armour restrictions.

2.7 Size limit – Robots must not exceed these dimensions. This includes all overhangs and weapons when in the retracted position *eg* an axe retracted may not exceed these limits; however in its "fired" position it may extend past these dimensions.
- Overall length 2 meters.
- Overall width 1.5 meters.
- Overall height 1.2 meters.

3. Mobility

3.1 Methods – All robots must have controlled mobility in order to compete. Methods of mobility include:
- *3.1.1 Rolling* – Rolling on wheels or the whole robot rolling.
- *3.1.2 Walking* – Walking such as linear actuator operated legs.
- *3.1.3 Shuffling* – Shuffling mechanisms such as rotational cam operated legs.
- *3.1.4 Ground effect* – Ground effect air cushions such as a hovercraft.
- *3.1.5 Jumping* – Jumping and hopping.

3.2 Restrictions – Robots are not permitted to use exposed rotating aerofoil, rocket or jet propulsion methods.

4. Radio control requirements

4.1 Frequencies

4.1.1 Regulation radio systems – Regulation radio systems used at *Robot Wars* MUST be commercially available and comply with restrictions put in place by local regulatory bodies and applicable laws.

4.1.2 Interference – Radio systems MUST NOT cause interference to other frequency users.

4.1.3 Allowed frequency – At *Robot Wars*, only the 2.4ghz DSS (Digital Spread Spectrum) frequencies are allowed for controlling your robot. Please see rule 4.4 regarding exceptions for telemetry systems.

4.2 Failsafes

4.2.1 Dangerous systems – All systems that are deemed to be "dangerous" (normally the drive and weapons) must have a "failsafe" device. This MUST bring the systems to a pre-set "off" or "zero" position if the transmitter signal experiences interference or is lost. These devices should also failsafe when the receiver battery is low or if power is completely lost.

4.2.2 Types of devices – The failsafe(s) may take the form of plug-in commercial devices; electronic circuitry incorporated into receivers or other devices. It could also consist of digital switches, which return to pre-set off position on loss of power. Care should be taken in the selection of devices to ensure they meet the requirements specified above.

4.3 Operation – All device(s) MUST operate to the tech checker's satisfaction before the robot will be allowed to compete.

4.4 Telemetry – Radio telemetry is permitted on 433MHz and 2.4GHz. Please notify *Robot Wars* if you are using radio telemetry.

5. Autonomous/ semi- autonomous robots

Robots that do not require human input for one or more of their functions.

If you are bringing an autonomous robot or a robot with significant autonomous functions, please contact *Robot Wars* in advance.

5.1 Remote operation – Any autonomous function of a robot, including drive and weapons, must have the capability of being remotely armed and disarmed.

5.2 Disarming – While disarmed, the robot is not allowed to function in an autonomous fashion.

5.3 Light – In addition to the required main power light, robots with autonomous functions must have an additional clearly visible light, which indicates whether or not it is in autonomous mode.

5.4 Deactivation – When deactivated the robot should have no autonomous functions enabled, and all autonomous functions should failsafe to "off" if there is loss of power or radio signal.

5.5 Timeout – In case of damage to components that remotely disarm the robot, the robot will automatically deactivate four minutes after being activated.

6. Electrical Power

6.1 Deactivation – All robots must incorporate a way of removing all power to weapons and drive systems (systems that could cause potential human bodily injury) that can be activated easily without endangering the person turning it off.

6.1.1 Removable link – The main power cut-off MUST be a removable link, which must NOT be in place unless the robot is in the arena, test arena or under the supervision of *Robot Wars* officials. A key or switch is not permitted. If there is more than one link they must be positioned adjacent to each other. All links must be removable by hand. The requirement to use a tool to remove the link is not permitted.

6.1.2 Accessibility – The link must be positioned in a visible part of the robot's bodywork which is accessible for a *Robot Wars* marshal when standing behind the arena barrier. The link must be fitted away from any operating weaponry or drive, and this position must be clearly marked.

6.1.3 Covers – The link may be fitted under a cover, but the cover must be able to be opened without the use of tools.

6.1.4 Kill switch – If the robot uses an internal combustion engine(s), the "Power" cut-off must take the form of a clearly labelled "Kill" switch. See Section 7 for further details on engines.

6.1.5 Inverted link – Robots that are capable of being driven inverted, having a removable link fitted that is only accessible when the robot is the right way up, must have a duplicate link fitted in the opposing panel, so as to allow the robot to be disarmed when inverted.

6.2 Cabling – Cabling must be of sufficient grade and suitably insulated for maximum operational current.

6.3 Exposed components – Current must not be carried through exposed components.

6.4 Power light – All robots must have at least one surface-mounted non-filament power light that is illuminated when power is supplied to the robot (*ie* when the link is in). The power light can be any color but must be non-flashing and be in contrast with its surroundings. All lighting on the robot, including power light or aesthetic lighting, must be powered through the removable links to ensure all lights are off when the removable link is removed.

6.5 Activation – The robot must be able to be activated and de-activated by way of the removable link from outside the arena.

6.6 Voltages – Voltage must not exceed 75V for direct current or 50V for alternating current. Note that batteries may have a higher voltage during charging and care must be taken not to exceed these limits.

7. Batteries

For assistance in selecting batteries please contact Robot Wars.

7.1 Protection – Batteries must be adequately protected within the body shell and securely fixed to minimize the chance of being punctured or coming loose during combat. In addition, packing such as high-density foam is recommended to reduce the shock of impacts.

7.2 Terminals – Battery terminals must be protected to prevent short circuits.

7.3 Permitted types – The only permitted batteries are ones that cannot spill or spray any of their contents when inverted. Standard car and motorcycle wet cell batteries are prohibited.

7.4 Approved battery chemistry – NiCd (nickel-cadmium); NiMH (nickel-metal hydride); Pb (sealed lead acid); LiFePo4 (lithium iron phosphate); LiPo (lithium polymer)

7.5 Parallel cells – Batteries' cells may be connected in parallel to increase capacity and discharge current. Caution must be taken with NiCd and NiMH as these cells may only be connected in parallel during discharge.

7.6 Charging – Improper charging may result in fire and/or explosion.

> **7.6.1 Design** – Only chargers specifically designed for the battery chemistry may be used. Chargers will be inspected during the Tech Check to ensure correct operation.
>
> **7.6.2 Rate of charge** – The rate of charge must not exceed the manufacturer's specification.

7.7 Pb (SLA), NiCd, NiMH and LiFePo4 – The following battery types can be used without any specific precautions although care must be taken with any battery particularly during charging:

> Pb (Sealed Lead Acid, SLA), non-spillable gel type (*eg* Yuasa, Hawker)
>
> NiCd and NiMH
>
> LiFePo4 (lithium iron phosphate)

7.8 LiPo batteries – Lithium polymer batteries have specific limitations and extra precautions which must be adhered to.

> **7.8.1 Charging** – LiPo batteries MUST be balance charged to prevent damage occurring to the cells. Chargers that do not incorporate an integrated balancing circuitry are not permitted.
>
> **7.8.2 Voltage cut-out (advisory)** – The robot should be fitted with an under voltage cut-out or alarm set at or higher than the battery manufacturer's recommendation to prevent the batteries from becoming damaged by over-discharge.
>
> **7.8.3 Fusing** – A fuse rated below the maximum burst discharge of the battery MUST be fitted.
>
> **7.8.4 Extra equipment** – Roboteers using LiPo batteries must provide a LiPo sack.
>
> **7.8.5 Inspection** – LiPo batteries must be removed from the robot, inspected and placed into a LiPo sack prior to and during the charging process.
>
> **7.8.6 Charging** – Lithium batteries must not be left unattended at any time during the charging process. Leaving batteries unattended while charging will be considered a serious breach of pit safety and may result in you and your robot being removed from the event. *Robot Wars* may provide a dedicated area for charging.
>
> **7.8.7 Damage** – LiPo batteries showing any evidence of damage or swelling must immediately be placed in a LiPo sack and removed to a safe, well ventilated area such as outdoors.

8. Internal combustion engines

8.1 Fuel capacity – Fuel capacity is limited to 500 ml (17 fl oz).

8.2 Fuel tanks –

> **8.2.1 Plastic** – Plastic fuel tanks separate to the engine must be made of an acceptable type of plastic (*eg* nylon).
>
> **8.2.2 Metal** – If the tank is integral to the engine assembly and is metal, the cap must be plastic or a plastic "pop off" seal fitted.
>
> **8.2.3 Protection** – The tank must be adequately protected from puncture.

8.3 Fuel lines – All fuel lines must be of the correct type and held with the correct type of fittings. They must be routed to minimize the chances of being cut.

8.4 Return spring – A return spring must be fitted to the throttle of all internal combustion engines to return the throttle to "idle" or "off" in the case of servo breakage or failure. This is in conjunction to any failsafe device.

8.5 Clutch – The output of any engines connected to weapons or drive systems must be coupled through a clutch which will de-couple the motor when it is at idle.

8.6 Remote shut-off – All engines must have a method of remotely shutting off.

8.7 Leaks – Any robot with liquid fuel and oil should be designed not to leak when inverted.

8.8 Non-standard types – Use of internal combustion engines other than standard piston type (*eg* turbines etc) are prohibited.

9. Pneumatics

9.1 Allowed gases – Pneumatic systems must use carbon dioxide [CO_2] or air.

9.2 Maximum pressure – The maximum pressure at any point within a pneumatics system must not exceed 1,000psi (68 bar).

9.3 Cylinders – The compressed gas shall be stored in a commercially manufactured gas cylinder of appropriate design, specification and certification, except where the maximum storage pressure is less than 50psi (3.4 bar).

9.4 Burst disc – The gas cylinder must incorporate a burst disc rated below the maximum test pressure of the bottle, except where the storage pressure is less than 50psi (3.4 bar).

9.5 Manual isolation – Valve gas cylinders charged to pressures of greater than 50psi must incorporate a manual isolation valve that can be operated from outside of the robot without the use of tools except for a 17 mm socket. Where the manual isolation valve is not integral to the gas cylinder (for example: the gas is normally released as soon as the cylinder is screwed into its mating pneumatic connection) [it] must have a manual isolation valve immediately after the cylinder which is accessible from outside of the robot.

9.7 Rating – All pneumatic components used with pressures greater than 50psi (3.4 bar) must be rated or tested to at least the maximum pressure available in that part of the system. You may be required to provide documentation or certification to support this.

> **9.7.1 Custom components** – Custom-made components, or parts operating above the supplier's maximum working pressure, must be independently tested and certified at 120% of the maximum system pressure available at that point.

> **9.7.2 Hydraulic components** – Components originally designed for hydraulics use will be de-rated by 50% for pneumatics use.

9.8 Pressure relief device – A certified pressure relief device must be installed in each part of the pneumatics system where a different operating pressure is used.

> **9.8.1 Rating** – Pressure relief devices must have a rating of 1,000psi (68 bar) or 110% of the pneumatic component with the lowest "maximum working pressure" rating protected by that particular pressure relief device, whichever is the lower.

> **9.8.2 Low-pressure systems** – Pneumatic systems employing pressures less than 50psi or systems employing air compressors that have a maximum output pressure lower than the pneumatic component with the lowest "maximum working pressure" do not require a pressure relief device. The pressure relief device(s) dictate the maximum pressure available in that part of the pneumatics system. The pressure relief device(s) must have a flow rate capacity that exceeds the maximum flow rate that can be expected under "over pressure" conditions. Any attempt to falsify the pressure settings of pressure relief device(s) will be considered as gross misconduct by *Robot Wars* and may result in expulsion.

> **9.8.3 Full pressure systems** – Non-regulated pneumatic systems or pneumatic systems where the regulator is not directly attached to the gas cylinder require that a 1,000psi pressure relief device is fitted.

> **9.8.4 Regulated systems** – Regulated pneumatic systems that operate at less than 235psi (16 bar) and where the regulator is directly attached to the gas cylinder do not require a 1,000psi pressure relief device before the regulator. The regulator must be rated to 120% of the gas bottle burst disc pressure. A pressure relief device is required downstream of the regulator rated at 110% of the component with the lowest "maximum working pressure" rating.

9.9 Pressure relief devices – Pressure relief devices should be readily accessible and must be removable for testing purposes.

9.10 Mounting – All pneumatic components must be securely mounted and adequately protected within the body shell. Any component storing gas (*ie* gas cylinders, buffer tanks etc) must be secured in such a way as it cannot escape the robot even if suffering a rupture.

9.11 Gauges – Pneumatic pressure gauges and pressure test points are not a requirement.

9.12 Dump valve – All pneumatic systems must incorporate a pressure dump valve which is easily accessible from outside of the robot without the use of tools. This dump valve shall quickly and reliably exhaust all gas downstream of the gas cylinder isolation (or remote isolation) valve including systems with a maximum operating pressure of less than 50psi (3.4 bar). If a system requires multiple dump valves, they must be located next to each other and securely mounted.

> **9.12.1 Normally open** – The dump valve shall be left open at all times when the robot is not in the arena or testing areas. Particular attention should be made that where non-return or quick exhaust valves are used, no part of the system is left pressurised.

9.13 Removable cylinders – Gas cylinders must be readily removable for inspection and refilling. You should ensure that your gas cylinder connection is compatible with *Robot Wars* filling stations.

9.14 Heaters and boosters – Pneumatic systems using heaters or pressure boosters are not permitted. Heating any pneumatic components, including prior to competition, is strictly prohibited.

9.15 Pressure equipment directive – Pneumatic components manufactured from June 1, 2002 shall carry a CE mark. Pneumatic components "custom made" since May 30, 2002 shall carry a label indicating their non-conformity with the "Pressure Equipment Directive" and their non-availability for sale. Components manufactured prior toMay 30, 2002 are not necessarily required to carry a CE mark.

10. Hydraulics

10.1 Pressure – Hydraulic system pressure (in the actuator or cylinder) must be limited to 10,000psi by way of a maximum pressure relief valve.

10.2 Test point – A hydraulic test point is a mandatory fitment to allow verification of a robot's maximum system pressure. A team will need its own test gauge and hose.

10.3 Storage tanks – Hydraulic fluid storage tanks must be of a suitable material and adequately guarded against rupture.

10.4 Standards – Hydraulic fluid lines and fittings must be to British Standard (BS) and/or to European DIN specifications.

10.5 Ratings – Hydraulic fluid lines and fittings must be capable of withstanding the maximum working pressures used within the robot.

10.6 Protection – Hydraulic fluid lines must be routed to minimize the chances of being cut or damaged.

10.7 Accumulators – Hydraulic accumulators (pressurized oil storage devices) are banned in whatever form they may take.

10.8 Power sources – Power sources may only be in the form of electric motors or petrol engines.

11. Rotational weapons or full body spinning robots

Full body spinning robots with an eccentric mass are excluded from this section unless they spin over 500 revolutions per minute.

11.1 Stopping time – The spinning element of any rotational weapon must spin down to a full stop in under 60 seconds.

11.2 Specifications – If you intend to create a rotational weapon you must provide the exact specification of the weapon in your *Robot Wars* application form. The requirements include the following:

- Weapon mass, including all rotating components such as gears and sprockets.
- Weapon rpm.
- Weapon diameter.

12. Springs and flywheels

12.1 Springs – Any large springs used for drive or weapon power must have a way of loading and actuating the spring remotely under the robot's power.

12.1.1 Deactivation – Under no circumstances should a large spring be loaded when the robot is out of the arena or testing area. These devices must be made safe before removing the robot from the arena or testing area.

12.1.2 Small springs – Small springs like those used within switches or other small internal operations are excluded from this rule.

12.2 Flywheels – Flywheels or similar kinetic energy storing devices must not be spinning or storing energy in any way, unless inside the arena or testing area. These devices must be made safe before removing the robot from the arena or testing area.

12.2.1 Remote deactivation – There must be a way of generating and dissipating the energy from the device remotely under the robot's power to allow safe activation and deactivation of the robot.

12.3 Failsafe – All springs, flywheels, and similar kinetic energy storing devices should fail to a safe position on loss of radio contact or power.

13. Weapon restrictions

The following weapons and materials are forbidden from use. Note: Some of the listed items may be allowed for effects but not as weapons. If you have an application of these items which you feel should be allowed, please include this in your application.

13.1 Invisible damage – Weapons designed to cause invisible damage to the other robot. This includes but is not limited to:

13.1.1 Electricity – Electricity as a weapon such as Tesla coils, Van-der-Graaf generators, stun guns, or cattle prods.

13.1.2 Radio frequency – Radio frequency jamming equipment or similar devices.

13.1.3 Radio frequency noise – Radio frequency noise generated by an IC engine. Use shielding around sparking components.

13.1.4 Electromagnetic fields – Electromagnetic fields from permanent or electromagnets which affect another robot's electronics.

13.2 Stopping combat – Weapons or Defenses which tend to stop combat completely, of both (or more) robots.

13.3 Rotating weapons – The speed of any rotating weapons – *eg* circular saws, carbon or steel cutting discs – must not exceed the manufacturer's specification. The manufacturer's specification must be available for inspection.

13.4 Hardened blades – Commercially manufactured hardened steel blades that may shatter are not allowed.

13.5 Untethered projectiles – Projectiles must have a tether capable of stopping the projectile at full speed and be no longer than 2.5 m.

13.6 Heat and fire – Heat and fire are forbidden as weapons. This includes, but is not limited to, the following:

> **13.6.1 Generated** – Heat specifically generated to damage an opponent.
>
> **13.6.2 Flammables** – Flammable liquids or gases.
>
> **13.6.3 Explosives** – Explosives or flammable solids such as DOT Class C devices, gunpowder, cartridge primers or military explosives, etc.

13.7 Smoke and light – Smoke and light-based weapons, which impair the viewing of robots by an entrant, judge, official or viewer. This includes, but is not limited to the following:

> **13.7.1 Smoke or dust** – Large quantities of smoke or dust. Limited smoke effects may be allowed.
>
> **13.7.2 Lights** – Lights such as external lasers and bright strobe lights, which may blind the opponent.

13.8 Hazardous materials – Hazardous or dangerous materials are forbidden from use anywhere on a robot where they may contact humans, or by way of the robot being damaged (within reason) contact humans. If unsure please contact *Robot Wars*.

14. Weapons additional

14.1 Weapon Restraints

> **14.1.1 Locking devices** – All high-speed weapons (*eg* all pneumatic and rotational weapons) must incorporate a secure restraint that locks the weapon in a safe position. The restraint may incorporate locking pins and bars but must be secured in such a way that it cannot be removed inadvertently. The design should ensure that the weapon cannot be fired during the activation process.
>
> **14.1.2 Positioning** – A locking device must be removable and re-insertable away from the line of fire and without the need for the Arena Marshal to contact any part of the robot.
>
> **14.1.3 Invertible** – Locking devices must be able to be fitted to a robot that is inverted or on its side without compromising rule 14.1.2.

14.2 Entanglement – Devices designed specifically to entangle other weapons are permitted under the following conditions:

> **14.2.1 Separation** – Entanglement devices must not cause two or more robots to be entangled together to the point where a battle requires intervention in order for it to continue.
>
> **14.2.2 Materials and construction type** – Any entanglement devices constructed with rope, wire, chain and similar materials may not be interlaced or woven. Nets, cloth, chainmail and similar are prohibited. For clarification on your device please contact *Robot Wars*.
>
> **14.2.3 Maximum length** – The maximum permitted length of rope, wire, chain and any similar materials is 1 m.

14.3 Interchangeable weapons – Robots with interchangeable weapons are permitted under the following conditions:

> **14.3.1 Weapon type** – All interchangeable weapons must comply with rule 12.1.
>
> **14.3.2 Weapon application** – All interchangeable weapons must be submitted on the *Robot Wars* application and are subject to approval.

For technical queries, rules clarifications and advice please contact Mentorn:
robotwarstechnical@mentorn.tv.

B – Previous winners

Full list of winners and runners-up from Series 1 to date.

Series	Winner	Grand Finalists		
1	Roadblock	Bodyhammer, Robot the Bruce, Recyclops, Cunning Plan, TRACIE.		

Series	Winner	Runner-up	Third place	Fourth place
2	Panic Attack	Cassius	Roadblock	Killertron
3	Chaos 2	Hypnodisc	Firestorm	Steg-O-Saw-Us
4	Chaos 2	Pussycat	Stinger	Hypnodisc
5	Razer	Bigger Brother	Firestorm 3	Hypnodisc
6	Tornado	Razer	Firestorm 4	TERRORHURTZ
7	Typhoon 2	Storm 2	Tornado	X-Terminator

Series	Winner	Runner-up	Grand Finalists	
8	Apollo	Carbide	TR2, Thor, Shockwave, Pulsar	
9	Carbide	Eruption	Ironside 3, Aftershock, Concussion, Apollo	

C — List of side competitions and winners

Championship	Winner	Runner-up
International League Championship	Razer (England)	Diotoir (Republic of Ireland)

Championship	Winner	Runner-up	Semi-Finalists	
First World Championship	Razer (England)	Behemoth (England)	101 (England)	Diotoir (Republic of Ireland)

Championship	Winner	Runner-up	Semi-Finalists	
Celebrity Special Championship	Pussycat (Adam Woodyatt)	Diotoir (Vic Reeves)	Gemini (Anthea Turner and Wendy Turner)	Sir Chromalot (Shane Lynch)

Championship	Winner	Runner-up	Third Place	Fourth Place
Tag Team Terror	King B3 and 101	Firestorm 2 and Scorpion	Bigger Brother and Plunderbird 4	X-Terminator 2 and Invertabrat

Championship	Winner	Runner-up
Annihilator North	Spikasaurus	Dominator 2
Annihilator South	Razer	Onslaught

Championship	Winner	Runner-up	Semi-Finalists	
War of Independence	Mortis (UK)	Frenzy (USA)	Ming 2 (UK)	Panic Attack (UK)
Second World Championship	Razer (UK)	Drillzilla (USA)	Manta (USA)	Tornado (UK)
The Forces	Anvil (Royal Air Force)	Mega-Hurts (Royal Navy)	Oblark (Fire Brigade)	Sub-Version (Submariners)

Championship	Winners		Semi-Finalists	
UK vs Germany	Fluffy (UK)	Das Gepäck (Germany)	259 (UK)	Delldog (Germany)

Championship	Winner	Runner-up	Semi-Finalists	
First European Championship	Tornado (UK)	Philipper 2 (Belgium)	Razer (UK)	Black Hole (Germany)

Championship	Winner	Runner-up
Annihilator	Kan-Opener	Ripper

Championship	Winner	Runner-up	Semi-Finalists	
All Star Championship	Pussycat	Dantomkia	Kat 3	Panic Attack
Third World Championship	Storm 2 (UK)	Supernova (Sri Lanka)	Crushtacean (South Africa)	Tough As Nails (Netherlands)

Championship	Winners		Runners-up	
Battle of the Stars	Arena Cleaner (Scott Mills and Chris Stark)	Kadeena Machina (Kadeena Cox)	The Cat (Suzi Perry)	Robo Savage (Robbie Savage)

D — Directory of competitor robots

Directory of competitors since the new generation of *Robot Wars*.
Note: The directory has been organized in alphabetical order and by series.

AFTERSHOCK — Series 9

Aftershock is built by the Shockwave team, who got to the Series 8 final. With a powerful vertical spinner, similar in power to Matilda's spinning blade, and angled armor to protect against other spinners, it's vulnerable to flippers, as it has no self-righting system.

Location	Reading and Gravesend.
Weapon	Vertical spinner.
Weight	110 kg.
Defense	The majority of the chassis is 6 mm hardened steel, with 15 mm hardened steel bulkheads; the top panels are 12 mm polycarbonate.
Top speed	13 mph.
Drive system	2 x brushed motors.
Power	Electric.
Battery	Lithium polymer, 10Ah.

AFTERSHOCK — Series 10

Aftershock was rebuilt for Series 10 and returned with four alternate weapons.

Location	Reading.
Weapon	30 kg, 2,400 rpm vertical flywheel plus alternative spinner bars: 14 kg double-edge bar, 18 kg single-tooth bar and a lighter 24 kg disc.
Defense	3 mm hardened steel with 15 mm hardened steel bulkheads; the top panels are 3 mm Hardox.
Weight	110 kg.
Top speed	14 mph.
Drive system	Four-wheel drive/1,000W 24V scooter motor.
Power	Electric.
Battery	Lithium polymer 6s, 20Ah.

ANDRONE 4000 — Series 10

Androne 4000 can apply 9 tons of force in 5 seconds using its hydraulic cylinder arm. However, its top armor is vulnerable to overhead axes.

Location	Marlow.
Weapon	Hydraulic cylinder arm that can match the size of the opponent. Maximum force of about 9 tons can be applied to opposing robot.
Weight	108.6 kg.
Top speed	15 mph.
Drive system	Two-wheel drive, NPC T64 gear motors rubber-mounted to custom mount brackets and puncture-proof 300 mm wheels.
Power	Electric and hydraulic.
Battery	4 x lithium polymer OptiPower 4s 5,000mAh 30c, 2 series, 4 parallel for 4 total, 34V.

APEX — Series 9

Apex's weapon is a 1,200 millimeter long, 1 inch thick hardened steel bar spinning at 1,750 rpm and using a motor at 58.8V. It has a top speed of 242 mph.

Location	Burntwood, Staffordshire.
Weapon	Spinner.
Weight	108 kg.
Defense	Hardened steel of various thicknesses. Front is protected by 8 mm, the flat sides have two plates of 10 mm, the sloped sides are 4 mm, the rear end protecting the motor is 6 mm and all the remaining hardened steel is 4 mm.
Top speed	18 mph.
Drive system	Two-wheel drive on a 5-to-1 gear ratio. Wheels are 6 inches in diameter using two AmpFlow E30-400 motors giving a top speed of approx 18 mph.
Power	Electric.
Battery	2 x 2.65Ah 6s for drive, 4 x 5Ah 7s wired to give 58.8V on the weapon.

APEX

Apex is a shuffler robot that moves using a system made of 14 legs. It also has three interchangeable bar weapons.

Location	Staffordshire.
Weapon	1,200 mm bar spinner using Mars ME0708 (Etek-R) with a speed of 1,750 rpm. Three interchangeable bars, 1,200 mm bar made from hardened steel (37 kg), single-tooth bar at 15 mm thick.
Weight	110 kg.
Defense	Wear-resistant steel (hardened steel) varying from 4 mm to 8 mm thickness.
Top speed	17 mph.
Drive system	Shuffler system, 14 legs, AmpFlow E40-400 motors on 24V.
Power	Electric.
Battery	Drive lithium polymer 6s, 22.2V. Weapon 58.8V 14s.

APOCALYPSE

Apocalypse has a secondary weapon in the form of grabbing arms that operate in addition to its pneumatic axe. Its grabbing arms exert 60 kilograms of force, and operate on around 6–8 bar (87–117psi).

Location	Coleshill, Warwickshire.
Weapon	4WD pneumatic axe.
Defense	Hardened steel, titanium and aluminium. Chassis comprises 20 mm tool plate aluminium.
Weight	110 kg.
Top speed	16.7 mph.
Drive system	AmpFlow A28-400 24V motors run using a Wotty 360A motor controller.
Power	Electric/pneumatic.
Battery	Lithium polymer 6s, 22.2V nominal.

APOLLO

Apollo is a wedge flipper robot powerful enough to launch a 100-kilogram competitor 6 feet into the air. It runs up to 1,000psi producing over 5.5 tons in force. With a limited supply of gas on board for the weapon, its main vulnerability is running out of firepower before the battle is over.

Location	North Wales.
Weapon	Flipper.
Weight	107.9 kg.
Defense	6 mm wear-resistant steel (front), 3 mm military grade steel.
Top speed	12 mph.
Drive system	2 x 1.2kW 24V motors, running through a two-stage chain-drive transmission.
Power	Pneumatic/electric.
Battery	Lithium polymer, 29V.

APOLLO

Series 8 champions, for Series 9 the Apollo team upgraded the power of the flipper weapon to 1,000psi full pressure and added a new 100-millimeter bore ram producing 5.5 tons of force.

Location	North Wales.
Weapon	Flipper.
Weight	107.9 kg.
Defense	Hardened steel, steel and high-density polyethylene.
Top speed	12 mph.
Drive system	Two 1.2kW 24V motors, running through a two-stage chain-drive transmission.
Power	Electric.
Battery	Lithium polymer, 29V.

APOLLO

Apollo returned for Series 10 with a completely rebuilt chassis and improved drive power.

Location	North Wales.
Weapon	100 mm bore full-pressure ram with 5.5 tons of force, an extra valve to increase the flow by 50%.
Defense	Laser-cut hardened steel.
Weight	110 kg.
Top speed	20 mph.
Drive system	AmpFlow A28-400-F48, 11hp each.
Power	Electric/pneumatic.
Battery	Lithium polymer, 48V.

BEAST

Whilst Beast's lack of armor leaves it vulnerable when under attack, its buffer tank technology enables it to efficiently use its gas supplies at a lower pressure, making it last longer.

Location	Lichfield, Staffordshire.
Weapon	Flipper.
Weight	109.9 kg.
Defense	"None as such" besides skeletal steel bars.
Top speed	10 mph.
Drive system	2 x 24V motors.
Power	Pneumatic/electric.
Battery	2 x lithium polymer, 25V.

BEHEMOTH Series 8

Robot Wars veterans Behemoth use a pneumatic lifting scoop, powerful enough to lift a Peugeot 205, to push around opponents. However, its thin side armor is an area of weakness.

Location	Hemel Hempstead, Hertfordshire.
Weapon	Pneumatic Lifting Scoop.
Weight	108.5 kg.
Defense	7 mm armor of Grade 5 titanium (weapon), with 3 mm stainless steel side armor.
Top speed	14 mph.
Drive system	Six-wheel drive, chain-driven, 2.5hp motors.
Power	Pneumatic, low-pressure (1,200kPa).
Battery	Lithium iron phosphate, 28V.

BEHEMOTH Series 9

For Series 9 Behemoth updated its weapon to be able to interchange between three different scoops depending on opponent. Other updates included drive and lifting power.

Location	Hemel Hempstead.
Weapon	Titanium scoop.
Weight	109.5 kg.
Defense	Titanium, polycarbonate and stainless steel armor.
Top speed	15 mph.
Drive system	Six-wheel drive, chain-driven, 5kW electric drive using LEM-130 and gripped rubber wheels.
Power	Electric/pneumatic.
Battery	Lithium iron phosphate A123, 28.8V.

BEHEMOTH Series 10

Behemoth returned for Series 10 with its interchangeable weapons including a pneumatic axe and anti-spinner scoop.

Location	Hemel Hempstead.
Weapon	Pneumatically driven lifting scoop, capable of lifting 250 kg.
Armor	Titanium, polycarbonate, stainless steel.
Weight	108.6 kg (with gas).
Top speed	15 mph.
Drive system	Six-wheel drive, chain-driven, electric drive using LEM-130 motors and high-traction rubber wheels.
Power	Electric/pneumatic.
Battery	Lithium iron phosphate A123, 28.8V.

BIG NIPPER Series 8

With a powerful crusher/gripper weapon, Big Nipper can pick up robots up to 300 kilograms. It has brushless motors to give it 300 kilograms of crushing power, as well as the ability to change its weapon to a 20-kilogram vertical spinning disc which can achieve 4,000 rpm in 5 seconds.

Location	Lancashire.
Weapon	Crusher, gripper, lifter and spinner.
Weight	110 kg.
Defense	Between 7 mm and 10 mm of Grade 5 titanium.
Top speed	20 mph.
Drive system	Eight-wheel drive powered by 2 x 10hp brushless motors.
Power	Electric.
Battery	Lithium polymer, 28V.

BIG NIPPER Series 10

Big Nipper's crusher weapon improved to 2.2 tons of crushing force.

Location	Lancashire.
Weapon	Crusher/grabber, interchangeable spinner.
Defense	Between 4 mm and 10 mm high grade titanium.
Weight	109.8 kg.
Top speed	18 mph.
Drive system	Eight-wheel-drive invertible system powered by 2 x 10hp modified brushless motors and electronics.
Power	Electric.
Battery	4 x packs of lithium polymer OptiPower ultra, 29.4V.

BONK Series 8

Bonk uses an efficient CO_2 gas system to reduce the "jump" experienced by other axe robots when engaging their weapon. This means effective use of the energy generated by their axe to maximize its impact on opponents.

Location	Stoke on Trent.
Weapon	Axe.
Weight	110 kg.
Defense	Wear-resistant steel, 8 mm front, 6 mm sides.
Top speed	17 mph.
Drive system	Four-wheel drive, 2 x 3hp motors.
Power	Pneumatic.
Battery	Lithium polymer, 26V.

BUCKY

Bucky has the capability to apply a third of a ton of biting force through its steel jaw crusher.

Location	Hayes, Middlesex.
Weapon	2 kg full pressure CO_2 steel toothed jaw crusher.
Defense	10 mm plastic sheet, 10 mm polycarbonate front scoop, steel chassis.
Weight	109.25 kg.
Top speed	18 mph.
Drive system	Two-wheel-drive, rubber buffer mounted 24V NPC T-64 gear motors over-volted to 34V, attached to 300 mm OD puncture-proof tires.
Power	Electric/pneumatic.
Battery	Lithium polymer OptiPower 4s 30c 8,000mAh, 80c Burst, 2 x in-series, 34V.

CARBIDE

The *Robot Wars* arena is one of the few in the world deemed safe enough to run Carbide's powerful 25-kilogram, 85-centimeter horizontal spinning bar.

Location	Derby.
Weapon	Spinning blade.
Weight	110 kg.
Defense	4.5 mm military grade steel/8 mm aerospace grade aluminium.
Top speed	12 mph.
Drive system	2 x 1.5hp electric motors.
Power	Electric.
Battery	Lithium polymer, 58.8V.

CARBIDE

Series 8 runner's up, Carbide made a complete overhaul of its internal components for Series 9, giving it enhanced reliability and power. These included an upgraded clutch assembly, new drive motors and a custom-made weapon motor allowing the horizontal bar to spin at 250 mph.

Location	Midlands.
Weapon	Spinner.
Weight	110 kg.
Defense	5 mm military grade steel, 8 mm aerospace grade aluminium and titanium.
Top speed	15 mph.
Drive system	2 x 4.3hp electric motors.
Power	Electric.
Battery	Lithium polymer, 58.8V.

CARBIDE

Arguably the most destructive *Robot Wars* competitor, Carbide returned for Series 10 with a refined design and the option of using a new interchangeable spinning bar.

Location	Midlands.
Weapon	Bar spinners with a tip speed of 240 mph.
Defense	5 mm military grade steel and 8 mm aerospace grade aluminium.
Weight	110 kg.
Top speed	Spinning bar tip speed 240 mph.
Drive system	Pair of AmpFlow 400 drive motors, 24V.
Power	Electric.
Battery	Drive system 8 cells (up to 33.6V). Weapon system 14 cells (up to 58.8V).

CHERUB

Cherub's main weakness is its exposed wheels, but it does have 360° rotating arms that assist it in escaping awkward situations in combat.

Location	Oxfordshire.
Weapon	Lifter.
Weight	101 kg.
Defense	All-steel, 8 mm thick at the front, 5 mm everywhere else.
Top speed	12 mph.
Drive system	750W Bosch motors. Ten to one gearbox 250 mm custom-made wheels.
Power	Electric.
Battery	Lithium polymer 6s, 22.2V.

CHIMERA

Another competitor with exposed wheels, this full-body axe robot is able to pivot on its axis. It's powered by two wheelchair motors and was built for a modest $2,150 budget.

Location	Bolton.
Weapon	Full-body axe.
Weight	72 kg.
Defense	An old gas canister, partially reinforced by steel, which varies from 10 mm at the front to 3 mm top and bottom.
Top speed	6 mph.
Drive system	2 x 24V wheelchair motors.
Power	Electric.
Battery	2 x sealed lead acid batteries, 12V.

CHIMERA 2   *Series 9*

For series 9 Chimera returned with interchangeable claw and axe weapons to defend against different types of opponent. Unlike the original robot, Chimera 2 was built with 1-inch high-density polythene plastic 18-inch wheels that can't be punctured.

Location	Bolton, Lancashire.
Weapon	Axe.
Weight	108 kg.
Defense	6 mm hardened steel armor.
Top speed	10 mph.
Drive system	2 x 800W 24V scooter motors with a stage-two 8:1 ratio gearing system.
Power	Electric.
Battery	Nickel cadmium, 24V.

CHOMPALOT   *Series 8*

Chompalot has a hydraulic-powered crushing weapon made from structural steel and is protected by 6-millimeter polycarbonate. It also has self-righting "wings" to defend against flipper opponents during battle.

Location	Derby.
Weapon	Crushing jaw.
Weight	99 kg.
Defense	6 mm polycarbonate.
Top speed	12 mph.
Drive system	2 x 24V 750W electric motors, double-reduction chain drive.
Power	Hydraulic.
Battery	4 x lithium polymer, 28V.

COBRA   *Series 9*

Cobra's four Movi-Motors drive system means it can reach 20 kph in under a second and has the ability to tow a truck.

Location	Belgium.
Weapon	Crusher.
Weight	110 kg.
Defense	3.2 mm hardened steel.
Top speed	20 mph.
Drive system	20 mph within one second and four Movi-Motors for drive.
Power	Electric drive/hydraulic weapons.
Battery	Lithium iron phosphate, 36V.

CONCUSSION   *Series 9*

Concussion was designed around its 6,000 rpm spinning drum weapon, machined from a single piece of hard steel for added strength and supported by a laser-cut, precision-welded frame.

Location	Wool, Dorset.
Weapon	Drum spinner.
Weight	109 kg.
Defense	Hardened steel side armor, polycarbonate top plate and aluminium base.
Top speed	18 mph.
Drive system	750W high-torque fixed magnet motors.
Power	3 x lithium polymer battery circuits, isolating the drive sides and the weapon motors as separate systems.
Battery	Drive 29.6V, weapon motors 22.2V.

CONCUSSION   *Series 10*

For Series 10 Concussion returned with an improved spinning drum, with the ability to hurl pieces of enemies out of the arena and cause internal damage.

Location	Dorset.
Weapon	26 kg drum spinner, 1.5 kg heavier than previous year.
Weight	110 kg.
Defense	Titanium, Raex hardened steel, polycarbonate.
Top speed	12–15 mph.
Drive system	Nano-tech Turnigy, AmpFlow F30-400 high-performance motors, Vex Victor BB ESC.
Power	Electric.
Battery	4 x lithium polymer nano-tech Turnigy 6.0Ah 25C-50c 6s, 22.2V.

COYOTE   *Series 9*

Coyote has electrically actuated gnarling jaws rated between 750–1,000 kilograms made from 10-millimeter wear-plate steel. Its chainsaw tail can spin at 3,000 rpm.

Location	Ayrshire.
Weapon	Crusher.
Weight	100 kg.
Defense	Steel and high-density polyethylene.
Top speed	15 mph.
Drive system	Two-wheel drive, driven by 24V 750W electric motors.
Power	Electric.
Battery	Lithium polymer, 22.2V.

COYOTE

Coyote returned for Series 10 with additional weapons including an electric chainsaw. Its jaws are powerful enough to lift a washing machine or a fridge.

Location	Ayrshire.
Weapon	Clamping jaws driven by an electric actuator rated for 750–1,000 kg, an electric chainsaw with a speed of 3,000 rpm and a mini thwack bot called Roadrunner.
Defense	22 mm copper pipe, 20 mm steel bar.
Weight	110 kg.
Top speed	12 mph.
Drive system	24V, 800W scooter motors with 6.25:1 gear ratio.
Power	Electric.
Battery	Lithium polymer 8Ah, 22.2V

CRANK-E

From the makers of Kill-E-Crank-E in Series 8, Crank-E is invertible and is armed with a central 22-kilogram vertical asymmetric spinner that rotates at 6,000 rpm.

Location	Caithness.
Weapon	Vertical spinner.
Weight	110 kg.
Defense	High-performance structural steel and wear-plate.
Top speed	Untested mph.
Drive system	Two-wheel drive, 2,750W brushless out-runners.
Power	Electric.
Battery	Lithium polymer, 44V.

CRACKERS N SMASH

This cluster bot is made up of 60-kilogram "Smash" and 50-kilogram "Crackers." Whilst the concept of using cluster bots makes the team vulnerable to flippers, Crackers benefits from a compact lifting weapon and Smash has a high mass spinner.

Location	North Yorkshire.
Weapon	Cluster bot.
Weight	Smash 60 kg, Crackers 50 kg.
Defense	Crackers has 5 mm of hardened steel with 3.6 mm hardened steel base; Smash has 3.6 mm hardened steel with 5 mm aluminium base.
Top speed	15 mph.
Drive system	Four-wheel drive with 100 mm wheels.
Power	Brushless electric motors providing 30kW.
Battery	Lithium polymer 12s.

CRAZY COUPE 88

A unique two-wheeled robot with front and rear rotating weapons. The front-facing 17-inch horizontal spinner rotates at 2,450 rpm while its rear vertical spinner acts as a lifter.

Location	Barnsley.
Weapon	Blade spinner on front with small rear disc spinner.
Weight	101 kg.
Defense	3 mm aluminium checker plate over Kevlar/carbon-fiber under-armor.
Top speed	8 mph.
Drive system	2 x 800W scooter motors.
Power	Electric.
Battery	8 x lithium polymer.

CRACKERS N SMASH

For Series 10 Crackers N Smash added an entanglement weapon consisting of single 1-meter lengths of steel cable connected in two places on a glass fiber rod.

Location	North Yorkshire.
Weapon	Smash: 13 kg Spinner functioning at 11,000 rpm with a tip speed of 250 mph. Crackers: 10kW lifting arm.
Weight	110 kg.
Defense	5 mm military grade and industrial grade hardened steel.
Top speed	18 mph.
Drive system	Four-wheel drive and 100 mm wheels. Both robots have 10kW peak of brushless electric power for drive systems.
Power	Electric.
Battery	Lithium polymer 12s, 44V.

CRUSHTACEAN

Crushtacean's claws have a 200-kilogram crushing force. Unlike some competitors it uses aluminium armor, as this material is more effective in absorbing impacts than alternatives such as hardened steel. Its claws are covered in polyurethane paint to protect them against spinners.

Location	Hale, Greater Manchester.
Weapon	Gripping claws.
Weight	100 kg.
Defense	Chassis 12 mm aerospace aluminium, domes 6 mm aerospace aluminium.
Top speed	20 mph.
Drive system	Two-wheel drive, 36V electric motors, claws driven by electric bottle jacks with 100 gm grip.
Power	Electric.
Battery	36V, 13Ah rated.

DANTOMKIA

Benefitting from quick acceleration, Dantomkia can quickly reach its maximum speed of 20 mph and rotate on the spot at 500 rpm.

Location	East Kirkby, Lincolnshire.
Weapon	Flipper/spinner.
Weight	108 kg.
Defense	Tank-armor grade steel.
Top speed	22 mph.
Drive system	750W/24V motor.
Power	Pneumatic.
Battery	Lithium polymer, 28.8V.

DISCONTRUCTOR

The high ground clearance of this robot makes it susceptible to flipper opponents. However, its stainless steel and titanium spinning disc features teeth designed to inflict maximum damage.

Location	Redhill, Surrey.
Weapon	Spinner.
Weight	103 kg.
Defense	6 mm Grade 5 titanium.
Top speed	15 mph.
Drive system	2 x 6-pole axial brush motors.
Power	Electric.
Battery	Lead acid, 24V.

DONALD THUMP

Donald Thump is a new competitor for Series 10 whose main weapon is a gold-colored vertical bar spinner.

Location	Hereford.
Weapon	Vertical spinner.
Weight	110 kg.
Defense	Overall 3 mm Hardox armor.
Top speed	14.95 mph.
Drive system	2 x AmpFlow E30-400 (2.1hp), totalling 4.2hp.
Power	Electric.
Battery	Lithium ion 24V for drive and lifter, lithium polymer 44V for spinner.

DRAVEN

Draven has a carbon-fiber and Kevlar composite shell with bonded-on titanium plates to produce armor that's designed to flex to cushion impact. However, should it flex too much it could cause one of its six drivechains to fail.

Location	Wiltshire.
Weapon	Crushing and lifting jaw.
Weight	110 kg.
Defense	Carbon-fiber and Kevlar composite shell with bonded-on titanium plates.
Top speed	15 mph.
Drive system	Six-wheel drive powered by twin 1,500W motors.
Power	Electric and hydraulic.
Battery	Lithium iron phosphate, 29.6V.

DRAVEN

For Series 9 Draven upgraded its weapon system to produce 6.6 tons of crushing force, half a ton of lifting force and a bite twice as fast as in Series 8.

Location	Wiltshire.
Weapon	Crusher.
Weight	106 kg.
Defense	4 mm solid titanium armour shell over carbon-fiber chassis.
Top speed	12–15 mph.
Drive system	8 x 800W brushed motors.
Power	Electric.
Battery	Lithium polymer.

ERUPTION

Eruption has the ability to launch its opponents up to 10 feet in the air and uses a custom-made control circuit to fire its weapon. Unlike other flipper robots, this system allows the amount of CO_2 to be altered for each flip, ensuring it'll never run out of CO_2 during a battle.

Location	Lymm, Cheshire.
Weapon	Flipper and gripper.
Weight	109 kg.
Defense	4 mm wear-resistant steel shell, 10 mm high-density polyethylene top impact absorbers, with an extra layer of 3 mm wear-resistant steel on its front.
Top speed	12 mph.
Drive system	2 x 750W motors with custom gearboxes.
Power	Pneumatic.
Battery	Lithium iron phosphate.

ERUPTION
Series 9

For Series 9 Eruption came back with interchangeable weapons, adding a vertical spinning disc and a crushing claw to its arsenal.

Location	Warrington.
Weapon	Flipper.
Weight	109 kg.
Defense	3–8 mm hardened steel shell with additional titanium and HDPE impact panels.
Top speed	12.6 mph.
Drive system	Two-wheel drive using 2 x Bosch GPA 750W.
Power	Drive: 25.9V. Weapon: full pressure CO_2.
Battery	Lithium polymer 7s 10Ah.

ERUPTION
Series 10

Eruption returned with an upgraded weapon system providing more pressure behind the claw plus a vertical spinner with a tip speed of 44 m/s.

Location	Warrington.
Weapon	Full-pressure pneumatic flipper (unregulated CO_2) plus crushing/gripping claw.
Weight	109.25 kg.
Defense	3.2 mm and 4 mm hardened steel shell and flipper arm, 10 mm absorbent panels on the top.
Top speed	Approximately 12.6 mph.
Drive system	Two-wheel drive, 2 x Bosch GPA 750W motors (one per wheel) and custom-built 4.6:1 gearboxes driving 2 x 150 mm caster.
Power	Electric/pneumatic.
Battery	Lithium polymer 5s 2,200mAh, nominal 18.5V.

EXPULSION
Series 9

Expulsion is notable for its unique weapon system – a half-meter spinning disc made of 10-millimeter military grade steel, which has four spikes hidden inside. The spikes only protrude once the weapon gets up to full speed, preventing opponents from trying to slow it down. The disc, which is protected inside the robot's body, has the ability to spin one way to slash the opponent and the other way to skewer it. The blades move at an impressive 20 times a second.

Location	Essex.
Weapon	Spinner.
Weight	105 kg.
Defense	3 mm steel plate sacrificial 'spaced armor'.
Top speed	5 mph.
Drive system	2 x 24V motors with worm gears giving high torque.
Power	Electric.
Battery	4 x 12V.

EXPULSION 2
Series 10

Expulsion 2 has potential to use a cluster bot and its armor can withstand machine-gun fire. However, its self-right mechanism isn't effective if the robot is flipped on to its weapon.

Location	Essex.
Weapon	Dynamic spinner with a tip speed of 92 mph.
Weight	Around 70 kg (this weight could allow for a cluster bot or extra armor).
Defense	Armox (stronger than Hardox) covered with rubber panels to absorb shock.
Top speed	15 mph.
Drive system	2 x 1kW motors running at 24V.
Power	Electric.
Battery	Lithium iron phosphate OptiPower 6s, 22V.

FOXIC
Series 8

Foxic's armor makes it one of the most solid *Robot Wars* competitors. It's a versatile robot with a lifting arm that can rotate backwards 270°.

Location	Bristol.
Weapon	Flipper/lifter/guillotine.
Weight	97 kg.
Defense	15 mm of wear-resistant steel.
Top speed	17 mph.
Drive system	2 x 5hp servo motors.
Power	Electric.
Battery	Lithium polymer.

FOXIC
Series 9

Foxic was rebuilt for Series 9 and came back with an interchangeable thicker arm for fighting spinners and hooks that could be substituted for the arm.

Location	Staffordshire.
Weapon	Flipper.
Weight	97 kg.
Defense	Between 6–20 mm of hardened steel.
Top speed	25 mph.
Drive system	4 x 5hp motors, 20hp total.
Power	Electric.
Battery	Lithium polymer 8s, 30V.

FROSTBITE
Series 9

Frostbite is a fully invertible robot made of tubular steel and 6-millimeter polycarbonate with a frosted design. It has a 600-millimeter spinning bar which runs at 2,000 rpm but is very light compared to other spinners.

Location	Kingston upon Thames.
Weapon	Bar spinner.
Weight	85 kg.
Defense	6 mm thick frosted polycarbonate.
Top speed	8–10 mph.
Drive system	Two-wheel drive, 24V mobility scooter gearboxes.
Power	Two 12V non-spillage gel car batteries.
Battery	Microlyte MRT 35Amh, 12V.

GABRIEL
Series 8

This robot has four interchangeable weapons – sword, battle-axe, pickaxe and sledgehammer. At 90 centimeters, each of Gabriel's wheels is as tall as a washing machine.

Location	Grove, Oxfordshire.
Weapon	Axe/hammer.
Weight	107.95 kg.
Defense	25 mm high-density polyethylene with a 6.2 mm steel armor plate.
Top speed	11 mph.
Drive system	Large electric motors.
Power	Electric.
Battery	2 x lithium polymer, 22.2V.

GABRIEL 2
Series 10

Gabriel 2 is one of the fastest robots in the arena and is capable of inflicting huge hits. It returned for Series 10 with an entanglement weapon.

Location	Oxfordshire.
Weapon	Mace with eight-point stars, sword, sledgehammer, double-hit hammer and entanglement rope for snagging.
Weight	110 kg.
Defense	6 mm Hardox 500 on the front, 4 mm Hardox and 20 mm HDPE top and bottom.
Top speed	17.5–20 mph.
Drive system	4 in AmpFlow motors.
Power	Electric.
Battery	Lithium iron phosphate 8s, 29.6V or 9s 33.3V.

GLITTERBOMB
Series 8

Glitterbomb has a powerful pneumatic axe with up to 1.3 tons of force behind it, and can strike at up to 120 mph. Its wheels are made from puncture-proof polyurethane foam and it has the ability to self-right from any position due to the strength and shape of its axe.

Location	Wrexham, North Wales.
Weapon	Axe.
Weight	105 kg.
Defense	3–4 mm Grade 5 titanium, cross-braced with 3 mm high-strength, wear-resistant steel.
Top speed	10 mph.
Drive system	2 x 24V motors, 4hp.
Power	Pneumatic weapon, electric drive.
Battery	4 x lithium polymer, 18.5V.

HEAVY METAL
Series 9

Heavy Metal's weapon is electrically powered and has an interchangeable tip to which a grabbing hook or saw can be added.

Location	Hinckley, Leicestershire.
Weapon	Rotating arm.
Weight	109.995 kg.
Defense	Steel chassis with Raex steel panels.
Top speed	12–15 mph.
Drive system	Bosch 750W brushed electric motor running at 28V.
Power	Electric.
Battery	Lithium polymer, 28V.

HIGH-5
Series 9

HIGH-5 is fully invertible and has a lifter weapon that can lift up to 280 kilograms. Its interchangeable rear drum spinner weighs 14 kilograms.

Location	Bristol.
Weapon	Lifter/spinner.
Weight	109.2 kg.
Defense	4 mm of hardened steel on top with two layers of 4 mm polycarbonate. The frame contains 6 mm of hardened steel on top with 30 mm steel tubing cross-member supports. Sides are 10 mm polycarbonate.
Top speed	12.4 mph.
Drive system	Two HP 24V motors.
Power	Electric.
Battery	2 x lithium iron phosphate 8,000mAh.

HOBGOBLIN   *Series 9*

Hobgoblin is the only "egg-beater" spinner ever to have entered the competition. It's a 20-kilogram vertical spinner that spins at approximately 2,500 rpm and has a diameter of 250 millimeters, creating a tip speed of 80 mph.

Location	Surrey.
Weapon	Spinning drum.
Weight	101 kg.
Defense	Frame is a mixture of water-cut high grade aluminium and hardened steel.
Top speed	9 mph.
Drive system	Hobgoblin runs a custom drivetrain. Power comes from 2 x 500W lawnmower motors.
Power	Electric.
Battery	Weapon and drive 4 x lithium polymer 6s, 22.2V. Receiver and weapon relay lithium polymer 3s, 11.1V.

HOBGOBLIN   *Series 10*

For Series 10 Hobgoblin's beater weapon was upgraded to 250 millimeters in diameter and a tip speed of 90 mph.

Location	Surrey.
Weapon	Unique egg-beater weapon, 20 kg mass spun at 2,500 rpm by a LEM170 brushed DC motor on 6s lithium iron phosphate.
Defense	High grade aluminium/HDPE plates/Hardox shell.
Weight	110 kg.
Top speed	12 mph.
Drive system	500W brushed DC motors.
Power	Electric.
Battery	Drive lithium iron phosphate 8s, 29.6V. Weapon lithium iron phosphate 6s, 22.2V.

INFERNAL CONTRAPTION   *Series 8*

Infernal Contraption features a vicious 16-kilogram, 10-millimeter-thick steel drum that spins at 1,000 rpm and flips back and forth as the robot accelerates. Infernal Contraption's body is made out of a sewage pipe, which doubles as plastic armor. Its wheels are old car tires.

Location	Cambridge.
Weapon	Spinner.
Weight	86.65 kg.
Defense	20 mm of sewage pipe.
Top speed	Untested mph.
Drive system	2 x 750W motors with custom gears.
Power	Electric.
Battery	Lithium iron phosphate.

IRON-AWE 6   *Series 10*

Iron-Awe 6's powerful flipping weapon is bolstered by added entanglement cannons.

Location	Bungay.
Weapon	High-pressured flipper supplied by 1 x 2 kg of CO_2 gas with 1,000psi pressure relief valve and an air cannon powered by low-pressure CO_2.
Defense	Body shell and flipper made of 3.2 mm hardened steel.
Weight	108.5 kg.
Top speed	12 mph.
Drive system	Two-wheel chain drive with 750W motors.
Power	Electric/pneumatic.
Battery	Lithium iron phosphate, 24V.

IRONSIDE 3   *Series 8*

Ironside 3 has a heavy, meter-long spinning bar weapon weighing 35 kilograms. The bar spins at 1,500 rpm. Due to the extreme gyroscopic effect that the blade achieves at full speed, the robot appears to "dance" and generate sparks every time it hits the floor.

Location	Nottingham.
Weapon	Spinner.
Weight	109 kg.
Defense	5 mm wear-resistant steel.
Top speed	12 mph.
Drive system	2 x brushed DC motors on 22V.
Power	Electric.
Battery	4 x lithium polymer, 22V.

IRONSIDE 3   *Series 9*

Ironside 3 returned for Series 9 with an improved motor to increase weapon speed and with a self-righting mechanism four times faster than previous versions.

Location	Nottingham.
Weapon	Spinning bar.
Weight	109 kg.
Defense	5 mm wear-resistant steel.
Top speed	12 mph.
Drive system	4 x brushed DC motors on 22V, 2 on the weapon and 2 on the wheels.
Power	Electric.
Battery	4 x lithium polymer, 22V.

JELLYFISH

Though Jellyfish is a relatively lightweight robot made from simple materials not usually associated with robot combat, it proved effective at grabbing and clamping its opponents in combat.

Location	Antrim, Northern Ireland.
Weapon	Clamp.
Weight	85 kg.
Defense	20–100 mm high-density polyethylene.
Top speed	15 mph.
Drive system	2 x E30-400-G AmpFlow motors.
Power	Electric.
Battery	Lead acid wired in series for 24V.

KING B REMIX

King B Remix is a flipper and ram-bot rebuilt using the best parts and philosophies from its previous incarnation, King Buxton.

Location	Portsmouth.
Weapon	Flipper and ram.
Weight	100 kg.
Defense	16 mm polycarbonate (top), manganese steel (front and rear), 16 mm ultra-high molecular weight polymer (rear).
Top speed	15 mph.
Drive system	Four-wheel drive from 2 x 1.8kW hand-wound motors.
Power	Electric.
Battery	Lithium iron phosphate, 40V.

KAN-OPENER

A powerful robot with 13 tons of crushing force, Kan-Opener is fully invertible and can work upside down.

Location	Northampton.
Weapon	Crusher.
Weight	108 kg.
Defense	3.2 mm wear-resistant steel reinforced with 8 mm aluminium on top panel.
Top speed	16 mph.
Drive system	2 x 750W motors running modified go-kart racing tires.
Power	Electric drive and hydraulic claws.
Battery	Lithium polymer, 25.9V.

MAGNETAR

From the team that brought Pulsar to *Robot Wars*, Magnetar is a drum spinner whose weapon generates enough gyroscopic power to flip the machine clean over.

Location	Shropshire.
Weapon	Drum spinner, tip speed of 250 mph.
Weight	107 kg.
Defense	8 mm thick Hardox 600, with areas of 6 mm and 3.2 mm Hardox 450.
Top speed	13.5 mph.
Drive system	4 x brushless skateboard motors, with optional magnetic downforce for additional traction.
Power	Electric.
Battery	Lithium iron phosphate 12s, ~50V.

KILL-E-CRANK-E

Kill-E-Crank-E's disc has three cobalt-edged bi-directional teeth. When attacking it brakes quickly when approaching its opponent, allowing momentum to flip it over to bring the spinner down forcefully in an arc on to its opponent.

Location	Caithness, Scotland.
Weapon	Vertical spinner.
Weight	108.7 kg.
Defense	8 in pipe of 304 grade stainless steel.
Top speed	9 mph.
Drive system	DC motors with two-stage gearboxes.
Power	Electric.
Battery	Sealed lead-acid, 24V.

MEGGAMOUSE

Meggamouse has 6-millimeter aluminium armor, which is an effective Defense against all weapon types. It also has a zero turning circle and can reach a top speed of 15 mph. Its minibot, called Charles, is designed to get far underneath opponents to get their wheels off the floor.

Location	Derby.
Weapon	Flipper/lifter.
Weight	105 kg.
Defense	6 mm aluminium armour and 4 mm hardened steel flipper.
Top speed	15 mph.
Drive system	2 x E30-400 AmpFlow motors. It has a unique four-wheel-drive system so it has a zero turning circle.
Power	Electric and pneumatic.
Battery	Lithium polymer, 22V.

M.R. SPEED SQUARED — Series 8

M.R. Speed Squared has an enormous full-body kinetic energy disc and interchangeable weapons that can be attached to the disc depending on their opponents' specific weakness.

Location	Worcestershire.
Weapon	Full 360° spinning wheel.
Weight	110 kg.
Defense	Rubber-mounted 3 mm aluminium over 3 mm steel frame.
Top speed	8 mph.
Drive system	2 x 0.75kW hospital trolley motors.
Power	Electric.
Battery	Lithium polymer.

M.R. SPEED SQUARED — Series 9

For Series 9 M.R. Speed Squared improved its top speed to 17 mph. Armor now consisted of a 100-millimeter hardened steel outer rim, two 10-millimeter tool steel cutting teeth and a steel inner carrier.

Location	Worcestershire.
Weapon	Full-body spinner rotating at 900 rpm.
Weight	108 kg.
Defense	Hardened and mild steel.
Top speed	17 mph.
Drive system	AmpFlow E30-400.
Power	Electric.
Battery	Lithium polymer 9s, 33V.

MS NIGHTSHADE — Series 9

Ms Nightshade is one of the tallest *Robot Wars* competitors. Its weapon consists of six petals with spikes surrounding the body, which acts as a hammer. The robot is designed to survive battle rather than inflict damage, and it has the ability to climb out of the Pit.

Location	Brighton.
Weapon	Spikes.
Weight	100 kg.
Defense	A mild steel shell on the inside of the petals to protect the main components when the petals are fully opened.
Top speed	Unknown.
Drive system	An internally communicated brush motor used to drive the wheels of two wheelchair motors.
Power	Electric and pneumatic.
Battery	2 x lead acid, 12V.

NUTS — Series 8

This two-wheeled robot with 1-kilogram weighted chains attached to each wheel attacks by spinning on the spot so the chains whip around with it to impact on its opponents.

Location	Reading.
Weapon	Flail chain and cluster bots.
Weight	110 kg.
Defense	Composite of 8 mm plastic with 3 mm wear-resistant steel.
Top speed	13 mph.
Drive system	High-power wheelchair motors.
Power	Electric.
Battery	Lithium iron phosphate.

NUTS 2 — Series 9

For Series 9, Nuts returned with an increased top speed of 20 mph, allowing its weapon to flail twice as fast as previously. It has three cluster bots that distract opponents.

Location	Hampshire.
Weapon	Flails.
Weight	102 kg.
Defense	6 mm hardened steel end caps with slanted edges to reduce biting points.
Top speed	20 mph.
Drive system	Two-wheel-drive brushed motors.
Power	Electric.
Battery	Lithium polymer, 24V.

NUTS 2 — Series 10

This cluster bot's Meltybrain circuits allow Nuts to spin and move at the same time.

Location	Somerset.
Weapon	Full-body flail spinner.
Weight	97 kg minus minibots, 110 kg combined.
Defense	6 mm plate steel and 3.2 mm chassis. Ring has been updated to 4 mm mild steel.
Top speed	26 mph. Minibots: 12 mph.
Drive system	A40-300 geared via stage 11:5:1 reduction to the 50 cm wheels.
Power	Electric.
Battery	Main bot 65 lithium iron phosphate 10Ah, 33.6V. Minibot lithium iron phosphate 3s and 6s, 12V and 24V.

ORTE

Orte features a double-skinned armor shell allowing it to continue fighting should one layer be damaged. It also has a powerful 10-centimeter piston ram weapon.

Location	Brighton.
Weapon	Flipper/rammer.
Weight	95 kg.
Defense	3 mm Grade 5 titanium.
Top speed	12 mph.
Drive system	Twin 750W motors with double chain-reduction system.
Power	Pneumatic/electric.
Battery	Lithium polymer, 29.6V.

OVERDOZER

Overdozer was the only Series 8 robot to be powered by a gas engine. It also featured non-conventional wooden fiberboard armor, making it more vulnerable to damage than its competitors.

Location	Falkirk.
Weapon	Spinning blade and fixed spikes.
Weight	86 kg.
Defense	18 mm medium density fibreboard.
Top speed	10 mph.
Drive system	2 x DC wheelchair motors, 24V.
Power	Electric.
Battery	Lithium polymer, 22.2V.

PP3D

A powerful spinner robot that unleashes 20kJ of energy at its weapon tip, which sits just millimeters from the arena floor. It's made up from 3D printed parts, a new approach not previously seen on *Robot Wars*.

Location	Aberdeenshire.
Weapon	Spinner.
Weight	108 kg.
Defense	6 mm wear-resistant steel, with 2 mm Grade 5 titanium top.
Top speed	12 mph.
Drive system	Details unavailable.
Power	Electric.
Battery	Lithium polymer, 32V.

PP3D

PP3D returned for Series 9 with a 31-kilogram horizontal spinning disc – one of the heaviest in the competition. The team has also mounted its drive motors on custom shock mounts to dampen the impact of any damage it inflicts on itself whilst attacking.

Location	Aberdeenshire.
Weapon	Spinner, 220 mph at disc tip.
Weight	110 kg.
Defense	3–6 mm wear-steel plate.
Top speed	15 mph drive.
Drive system	2 x T64 motors.
Power	Electric.
Battery	Lithium polymer.

PULSAR

With its signature siren-like sound, Pulsar featured the fastest drum flywheel weapon in Series 8, weighing 14.5 kilograms and rotating at up to 9,000 rpm (220 mph). The robot has a number of 3D printed components and has a unique modern sensorless brushless electric drive system normally used in large model aircraft.

Location	Shropshire.
Weapon	Spinning drum with metal teeth.
Weight	107 kg.
Defense	Front plate and chassis 8 mm wear-resistant steel, top and base plates 4.5 mm ultra-hard steel, polyethylene plastic wheel guards.
Top speed	15 mph.
Drive system	Modern sensorless brushless electric motors, custom two-stage reduction gearbox.
Power	Electric.
Battery	Lithium polymer, 50V.

PULSAR

Pulsar was completely redesigned for Series 9, although keeping its original shape and theme. It featured an upgraded drum weapon, weighing 24 kilograms with gearing for 8,700 rpm. Improved geometry and greater mass of the weapon gave it more consistent bite on opponents, transferring more energy more often.

Location	Shropshire.
Weapon	Drum spinner.
Weight	109 kg.
Defense	Hardened wear-plate steel. Frame, wedge and rear plate 8 mm thick, with 6 mm wheel-guards and 3.2 mm top and bottom panels. Also patches of 6 mm polycarbonate plastic to save weight and display the internals.
Top speed	15 mph.
Drive system	Rebuilt 50cc-equivalent brushless out-runners, originally intended for large model aircraft.
Power	Electric.
Battery	Lithium polymer 14.4Ah, 50V.

PUSH TO EXIT
Series 9

Push To Exit is the only front-hinge flipper in the series' main competition. It runs on low-pressure pneumatics and features a one-of-a-kind "Swan Drive" drive system that's easy to bolt on and off and makes the robot fast and agile.

Location	Mablethorpe, Lincolnshire.
Weapon	Flipper.
Weight	110 kg.
Defense	3–6 mm hardened steel.
Top speed	About 22 mph.
Drive system	AmpFlow A40-300 24V motors on to an 8:1 gearbox, all made into one drive pod. This "Swan Drive" is custom made, and will run at 28.8V.
Power	Electric.
Battery	4 x lithium polymer OptiPower 4s 8,000mAh.

PUSH TO EXIT
Series 10

Push To Exit returned for Series 10 with added entanglement capability and improved armor.

Location	East Kirkby, Lincolnshire.
Weapon	Front-hinge flipper running on 10 bar, with added buffer tanks for better performance.
Defense	Titanium, hardened steel and aluminium.
Weight	105.8 kg.
Top speed	About 22 mph.
Drive system	AmpFlow 24V DC motors geared to 25 mph. Custom drive.
Power	Pneumatic.
Battery	Lithium polymer OptiPower, 28.8V.

RAPID
Series 9

Rapid was a brand new competitor for Series 9 and stood out with its low profile and chrome paint. It has a flipper capable of lifting 7.7 tons, five times more powerful than opponents, and cost $35,000 to build.

Location	Central London.
Weapon	Flipper.
Weight	110 kg.
Defense	6 mm and 3.2 mm hardened steel with small high-density polyethylene panels and a 10 mm aluminium base plate.
Top speed	17 mph.
Drive system	Two high-performance fan-cooled AmpFlow A28-400-F4.
Power	Electric.
Battery	Lithium polymer, 42V.

RAPID
Series 10

Rapid is capable of flipping opponents high into the air, but its low ground clearance means it's susceptible to low-profile cluster bots.

Location	London.
Weapon	Rapid has customised pneumatics running at 60 bar with a 120 mm bore ram.
Defense	5 mm hardened steel, 12 mm polycarbonate, 20 mm HDPE side panels, hardened tool steel plate, solid steel spike pods and extra thick reinforced plastics for shock absorption.
Top speed	23 mph.
Drive system	20 hp and four-wheel-drive system with high spec AmpFlow 48V electric motors.
Power	Electric/pneumatic.
Battery	10-cell lithium polymer, 42V.

RAZER
Series 8

One of the most memorable and successful original *Robot Wars* competitors, Razer returned for Series 8 featuring its hydraulic piercer weapon, which applies nine tonnes of pressure.

Location	Bournemouth.
Weapon	Hydraulic piercer/lifter.
Weight	109 kg.
Defense	2.5 mm hardened steel, with a 5 mm shield.
Top speed	12 mph.
Drive system	Four-wheel drive, tank-track style.
Power	Hydraulic.
Battery	Lithium polymer, 12V.

RUSTY

Rusty is an old robot that was refurbished by students from Glasgow Clyde College to feature more modern components and materials for Series 9. The robot is a low-pressure flipper designed to be highly reliable and easy to maintain and run, as well as allow students to learn the basics of electronics, mechanics, fabrication, pneumatics, manufacture and design.

Location	Glasgow.
Weapon	Flipper.
Weight	108 kg.
Defense	3.2 mm hardened steel mounted on 10 mm of aluminium, 5 mm hardened steel scoop and 3 mm titanium flipper arm.
Top speed	14 mph.
Drive system	2 x AmpFlow E30-150 motors chain-driven to go-kart wheels.
Power	3 hp drive, 1,200 kg of lift on the flipper.
Battery	Lithium polymer, 22.2V.

SABRETOOTH

Sabretooth is unique in featuring three different weapons at one time: a 22 kg aluminium drum spinner (operating at 4,500 rpm), a flipper and a moveable gripper. The chassis consists of two layers of armor plate with HDPE, keeping it light and agile.

Location	Guildford, Surrey.
Weapon	Spinner, gripper and armored wedge.
Weight	106 kg.
Defense	A composite of wear-resistant steel and high-density polyethylene.
Top speed	8 mph.
Drive system	Four-wheel drive, 24V.
Power	Electric.
Battery	Lithium polymer, 30V.

SABRETOOTH

For Series 9, Sabretooth featured more innovative features including a 25 kg drum spinner reaching 7,000 rpm.

Location	Haslemere, Surrey.
Weapon	Drum spinner.
Weight	109 kg.
Defense	3 mm hard-wearing and wear-resistant steel plate and 4 mm ultra-hard steel plate armor.
Top speed	9 mph.
Drive system	Two T64 NPC 1.7 hp motors.
Power	Electric.
Battery	Lithium polymer, drum 44V, drive 28V.

SABRETOOTH

Sabretooth was rebuilt for Series 10, returning with a 22 kg spinning drum weapon.

Location	Haslemere, Surrey.
Weapon	22 kg spinning drum turning at 7,000 rpm.
Weight	106.85 kg.
Defense	3.2 mm Hardox and layered HDPE.
Top speed	15 mph.
Drive system	2 x AmpFlow A24-400 48V driven by VEX BB controllers.
Power	Electric.
Battery	Lithium polymer 12s Turnigy Graphene.

SHOCKWAVE

Shockwave has interchangeable weapons that allow lifterbot, with 200 kg of lifting force, to take on different types of opponents. Uses drive motors the same as those used on fairground carousel rides.

Location	Reading.
Weapon	Rotating lifting arm with multiple weapon choices (wedges/spikes/snow plough).
Weight	110 kg.
Defense	4 mm steel armor plating with 15 mm high-density polyethylene plastic.
Top speed	20 mph.
Drive system	2 x 4kW fairground ride motors driving 4 x go-kart wheels.
Power	Electric.
Battery	Lithium iron phosphate, 40V.

STORM 2

Storm 2 runs a live telemetry system during battles that shows the robot's performance and allows the team to make real-time strategy decisions as well as analyze battle results. Storm 2 is estimated to have cost $35,000 to build.

Location	Suffolk.
Weapon	Interchangeable.
Weight	107 kg.
Defense	Titanium armor plate, with extra-high-hardness protective steel.
Top speed	12 mph.
Drive system	Bespoke rare earth magnet PMDC motors.
Power	Electric.
Battery	Lithium polymer, 42V.

SUPERNOVA — Series 8

Supernova's spinner blade rotates at 2,500 rpm and is made from 22 kilograms of 12-millimeter steel. The sheer power of the disc means that the team are unable to test it outside a fully sealed combat arena.

Location	Wallington, Surrey.
Weapon	Spinning disc.
Weight	94 kg.
Defense	5–10 mm aluminium alloy.
Top speed	10 mph.
Drive system	2 x 1 hp motors
Power	Electric.
Battery	Lithium polymer, 50V.

SUPERNOVA — Series 9

For Series 9, Supernova returned with a 22-kilogram disc made from a single piece of hardened steel and armor four-times stronger than the previous series.

Location	Surrey.
Weapon	Spinner.
Weight	94 kg.
Defense	3–6 mm of hardened steel.
Top speed	12–15 mph.
Drive system	Two brushed motors.
Power	Electric.
Battery	Lithium polymer 12s.

SWEENEY TODD — Series 8

Sweeney Todd is the only *Robot Wars* competitor to use Mecanum wheels – a conventional wheel with a series of rollers attached to its circumference. This means is can move in every direction, not just forwards and backwards.

Location	Oxford.
Weapon	Spinner.
Weight	45 kg.
Defense	4 mm thick steel.
Top speed	10 mph.
Drive system	4 x 100:1 motors connected to wheels.
Power	Electric.
Battery	Lead acid, 12V.

TAURON — Series 9

Tauron is fully invertible, with a reversible vertical spinning-bar weapon. The weapon weighs 13 kilograms and is powered by a brushed DC motor running at 42V. Its pivoting design means it can operate its weapon at maximum lethality regardless of which way up it finds itself.

Location	Bedfordshire.
Weapon	Spinning drum.
Weight	110 kg.
Defense	6 mm and 4 mm military grade steel.
Top speed	12 mph.
Drive system	2 x 1.5 hp electric motors.
Power	Electric.
Battery	Lithium polymer, weapon 42V, drive 32V.

TAURON — Series 10

Tauron returned for Series 10 with an 18-kilogram, 600-millimeter vertical and reversible spinning bar.

Location	Bedfordshire.
Weapon	18 kg, 600 mm vertical reversible spinning bar, 50.4V, running at 3,600 rpm, tip speed 244 mph.
Defense	10 mm HDPE, Hardox 450 3.2 mm, Hardox 500 4 mm.
Weight	110 kg.
Speed	10–12 mph.
Drive system	2 x 1.5 hp NPC-T64 motors each running at 33V.
Power	Electric.
Battery	Lithium polymer 33V, lithium polymer 50.4V.

TERRORHURTZ · Series 8

TERRORHURTZ's polycarbonate armor is made from the same materials as the arena walls. It has the biggest axe weapon in the competition. At 90 centimeters long, the blunt titanium axe fires at 100 mph and is designed to bring maximum trauma to opponents' interior workings.

Location	Oxford.
Weapon	Double-ended axe.
Weight	107 kg.
Defense	6 mm wear-resistant steel with 12 mm polycarbonate.
Top speed	11 mph.
Drive system	2 x 1,000W, 24V motors.
Power	Pneumatic.
Battery	Lithium polymer, 26V.

TERRORHURTZ · Series 9

For Series 9 TERRORHURTZ returned with the team working on reliability issues that caused a disappointing performance in Series 8. The largest axe weapon in the series delivers a tonne of force on impact.

Location	Oxford.
Weapon	Double-headed axe.
Weight	106 kg.
Defense	6 mm folded wear-plate, 12 mm bullet-proof polycarbonate armor and steel.
Top speed	12 mph.
Drive system	Two-wheel drive, 24V 1,000W motors.
Power	Electric.
Battery	Lithium polymer.

TERRORHURTZ · Series 10

After the damage caused by Aftershock in Series 9, TERRORHURTZ rebuilt their chassis, refined the pneumatic system and added brand new armor for Series 10.

Location	Oxford.
Weapon	8 mm titanium double-headed pneumatic axe, operating at up to 120psi.
Defense	6 mm Armox 500, 12 mm polycarbonate.
Weight	103.6 kg.
Top speed	11 mph.
Drive system	Two-wheel drive, 52V Bosch GPA 400 motors, 1,500W each.
Power	Electric/pneumatic.
Battery	Lithium polymer 14s.

TERROR TURTLE · Series 8

Terror Turtle runs with thinner armor compared to its competitors but has a cluster bot, "The Hatchling." The main robot runs a 9-kilogram, 3,000 rpm spinner while The Hatchling is designed to ram other robots but doesn't have an active weapon.

Location	Lewes, Sussex.
Weapon	Spinner/cluster bot.
Weight	Main robot 86 kg, The Hatchling 21.5 kg.
Defense	Main robot 4 mm fiberglass (top), 2 mm aluminium (front sides), 4 mm steel box, The Hatchling 3 mm mild steel throughout.
Top speed	Main robot 5 mph, The Hatchling 20 mph.
Drive system	Main robot heavy-duty wheelchair gearboxes and motors, The Hatchling industrial electric drills.
Power	Electric.
Battery	Drive uses nickel-metal hybrid battery, 28.8V. Weapon lithium polymer, 25.9V. The Hatchling nickel-metal hybrid, 28.8V.

THE GENERAL · Series 8

A four-wheel-drive rammer robot, The General has two front-mounted vertical spinning discs. Its design is based on a tank and is made from many parts found around the farm where the team is based.

Location	Carmarthen, South Wales.
Weapon	Rammer/vertical spinning discs.
Weight	110 kg.
Defense	2.5 mm aluminium.
Top speed	15 mph.
Drive system	Four-wheel drive, powered by two large electric gate motors, 24V.
Power	Electric.
Battery	Sealed lead-acid, 24V.

THE KEGS · Series 10

The Kegs are a pair of 50-kilogram robots, each armed with 10-kilogram spinning bars. The two auxiliary robots are wedge-shaped doorstops designed to sneak under opponents and disable them.

Location	Lewes.
Weapon	2 x 10 kg spinning bars.
Defense	The Kegs are made of 2.5 mm curved stainless steel from an old beer keg.
Weight	109 kg combined.
Top speed	12 mph.
Drive system	24V, 350W Unite electric bike motors.
Power	Electric.
Battery	Drive nickel-metal hydride, 24V. Weapon lithium polymer, 29.6V.

THERMIDOR 2 — Series 8

Thermidor's pneumatic flipper can lift 2,300 kilograms and can run upside down, using the flipper to self-right.

Location	Norwich.
Weapon	Flipper.
Weight	110 kg.
Defense	5 mm polycarbonate flipper and sides, 3 mm aluminium cover, 5 mm mild steel top cover, 2 mm mild steel claws.
Top speed	15 mph.
Drive system	2 x 750W motors.
Power	Pneumatic.
Battery	Lithium polymer, 25.9V.

THE SWARM — Series 10

The Swarm is a cluster collection of four bots each having its own weapon.

Location	Brighton.
Weapon	Pincers/flipper/spinner/anti-spinner.
Defense	Hardox 3.2 mm.
Weight	The four bots are 24.5 kg, 23.5 kg, 27 kg and 29 kg.
Top speed	Unknown.
Drive system	The drive systems use Saturn16 gearboxes, driven by an RB 775 18V motor and a 1.5:1 reduction done with sprockets and chains.
Power	Electric.
Battery	Lithium polymer, 18.5V.

THOR — Series 8

Thor's low-pressure pneumatic axe improves its reliability whilst being extremely powerful. A demonstration of this power saw Thor smash up a caravan, and it can easily tow a 1-ton car, meaning it has the capacity and width to push two robots around at once.

Location	Northampton.
Weapon	Axe/hammer.
Weight	105 kg.
Defense	Aluminium and wear-resistant steel.
Top speed	30 mph.
Drive system	8 hp electric motors.
Power	Pneumatic.
Battery	Lithium polymer, 28V.

THOR — Series 9

For Series 9 Thor made improvements to its armor and chassis design. This led to a much more compact robot with a flatter front so that it could get underneath opponents. It also has the option of using interchangeable armor panels.

Location	Northampton.
Weapon	Axe.
Weight	105–108 kg.
Defense	Hardened steel and aluminium.
Top speed	30 mph.
Drive system	Mag motors.
Power	Electric for drive and pneumatic.
Battery	Lithium.

THOR — Series 10

For Series 10 Thor's weapon system has been improved to fire twice as fast as previous versions. It also has entanglement ability using steel rope or barbed wire. It remains one of the fastest robots in the competition.

Location	Northampton.
Weapon	Hammer powered by 2 x 2 kg CO_2 with four regulators, with newly designed weapon arm with five interchangeable hammers.
Weight	106.5 kg.
Defense	6 mm Hardox, 3 mm Hardox and aluminium.
Top speed	30 mph.
Drive system	Two-wheel drive with c40 Mag motors giving 32 hp, along with custom-made wheels designed especially for Thor.
Power	Electric/pneumatic.
Battery	Lithium polymer 7s, 28V.

TMHWK — Series 9

TMHWK has interchangeable axe heads, including a wedge-shaped axe, and an attachable scoop. One axe is used for grabbing opponents whilst the other is used for piercing tires. The scoop enables them to hold opponents in place at the same time as attacking with the axe.

Location	Netherlands.
Weapon	Axe.
Weight	106 kg.
Defense	3.2 mm hardened steel and 15 mm high-density polyethylene.
Top speed	Untested mph.
Drive system	GPA 750 motor.
Power	Electric.
Battery	Lithium polymer 8s.

TOUGH AS NAILS
Series 8

Tough As Nails' crusher unleashes 1.3 tons of force on opponents caught between its pincers. The width of the robot allows it to wrap its weapon around robots for maximum crushing effect.

Location	Helvoirt, Netherlands.
Weapon	Crusher.
Weight	107 kg.
Defense	3.2 mm high-grade wear-resistant steel.
Top speed	10 mph.
Drive system	2 x 3,000W motors.
Power	Electric/pneumatic.
Battery	Lithium polymer.

TR2
Series 8

A powerful flipper, TR2 has an additional axe weapon on the rear that works in tandem with the flipper. The weapons exert about 1 ton of force when activated.

Location	Gateshead, Tyneside.
Weapon	Flipper and axe.
Weight	105.35 kg.
Defense	3.2 mm wear-resistant steel, with 20 mm high-density polyethylene panels.
Top speed	15 mph.
Drive system	750W motors with custom-made gearbox.
Power	Pneumatic.
Battery	4 x lithium iron phosphate, 26V.

TRACK-TION
Series 10

Track-Tion's crushing arm exerts 600 kilograms of force and its armor includes novel use of a chopping board.

Location	Surrey.
Weapon	Crusher/gripper steel claw with a force of approximately 600 kg.
Defense	Chassis: 3 mm mild steel. Armor: layered 3/5 mm mild steel and 5 mm aluminium plus a chopping board.
Weight	95 kg.
Top speed	10 mph.
Drive system	2 x CIM motors 17:1 Maxon planetary gearboxes, driving 2 x 5,000mAh, 7s Turnigy heavy-duty lithium polymer packs.
Power	Electric.
Battery	Lithium polymer 7s 2,5000mAh packs in parallel.

TROLLEY RAGE
Series 9

Trolley Rage uses recycled components, which helps to keep build costs down. It's constructed from an upturned shopping cart and its motors were taken from a wheelchair. It also has two interchangeable weapons – mounted spikes or a wedge.

Location	Medway, Kent.
Weapon	Axe.
Weight	108 kg.
Defense	3 mm steel plating.
Top speed	6 mph.
Drive system	2 x 24V wheelchair motors.
Power	Electric.
Battery	2 x lithium ion, 21V.

VULTURE
Series 10

Vulture's axe can travel 180° in half a second, exerting 1,200 newtons of force.

Location	Newcastle.
Weapon	Spinning bar head 300 mm in diameter, geared for 6,000 rpm, and an axe.
Defense	6 mm wear-plate steel with 8 mm panels.
Weight	100 kg.
Top speed	16 mph.
Drive system	Two-wheel drive using one 24V, 1,600W motor per side through a three stage chain gearbox to the wheels.
Power	Electric.
Battery	8s lithium polymer, 30V.

WYRM
Series 9

Wyrm uses ultra-high molecular weight polyethylene (UHMWPE) armor on its sides, top and bottom. Similar to the materials used in the arena walls, UHMWPE has high abrasion resistance.

Location	Falkirk.
Weapon	Lifting wedge.
Weight	110 kg.
Defense	10 mm hardened steel.
Top speed	13 mph.
Drive system	2 x 1,000W electric scooter motors totalling about 2.7 hp.
Power	Electric.
Battery	3 x lithium polymer 3s, 33V.

Robot Wars information

www.robotwars.tv – The official Robot Wars website.
www.robochallenge.co.uk – The technical team behind Robot Wars, and the
    authors of this manual.

Robot Wars social media

Official Robot Wars Twitter – @UKRobotWars.
Official Robot Wars Facebook – UKRobotWars.
Robo Challenge Twitter – @RoboChallenge.
Robo Challenge Facebook – RoboChallenge.
Official Carbide Facebook – CarbideRobot.
Official Eruption Facebook – EruptionRobot.
Official TERRORHURTZ Facebook – Terrorhurtzrobot.
Official Apollo Facebook – ApolloRobot.
Official Pulsar & Magnetar Facebook – teamranglebots.
Official Gabriel Facebook – teamgabrielrobot.
Official Nuts Facebook – nutsrobotics.

Acknowledgements

Grant and I would like to sincerely thank a number of people who helped make this book possible. Firstly Nick Cooper, our father, whose unwavering support from our early years onwards has made it possible for us to enjoy an amazing, creative and challenging career. Thank you, Dad!

We're also extremely grateful to Marc Thorpe, the inventor of *Robot Wars*, not only for his creative genius and get-go attitude which brought this hobby to life, but also for his generosity in sharing with us the story of how *Robot Wars* was born.

We'd also like to thank the many roboteers and teams from the world of robot combat whom we regard as our good friends. In particular we'd like to thank John Reid from TERRORHURTZ, Alan Young from Apollo and my wife Helen Cooper for their special contributions to the book. We're also grateful to Sam Smith and Dave Moulds from Carbide, Ian Lewis from Razer, Ellis Ware from Magnetar, Michael Oates from Eruption, Andrew Marchant from Tornado, Craig Collias from Gabriel, Rory Mangles from Nuts, and Adam Turner, for their valuable contributions.

Finally we'd like to say a big thank you to our friends at Mentorn for bringing *Robot Wars* to our screens and, most importantly, for believing in our ability to be involved as the technical consultants.

Thank you.

James and Grant Cooper
August 2017

Authors

James and Grant Cooper were inspired from an early age by the original *Robot Wars* television program, and with encouragement and support from their father, Nick, later formed Robo Challenge Ltd, based in Birmingham, serving a range of clients, including *Robot Wars*, to design and produce creative engineering projects, primarily for television shows and PR campaigns. Today, they enjoy the creative problem solving required to tackle many and varied new projects – skills that were nurtured during their early days building combat robots.

Nick, Grant and
James Cooper.

android A robot that looks like a person.

burr A rough area on a piece of metal that is left after the metal is cut.

chamfer The surface formed by cutting away the angle at the intersection of two faces of a piece of material.

fitment Equipment or fittings.

flywheel A heavy wheel that is part of a machine and that controls the speed of machinery.

formidable Large or impressive in size, power or strength.

gravimetric Measured by weight.

hydraulics The science that deals with ways to use liquid when it is moving.

kinetic Of or relating to the movement of physical objects.

lathe A machine in which a piece of wood or metal is held and turned while being shaped by a sharp tool

locomotion The act or power of moving from place to place.

monocoque The structure of a vehicle in which the body shares the stresses with the chassis.

pneumatic Using air pressure to work.

solder To join something with something else using a mixture of metals.

For More Information

FIRST Robotics Competitions
200 Bedford Street
Manchester, NH 03101
Phone: (800) 871-8326

Website: https://www.firstinspires.org

Twitter: @FIRSTweets

FIRST robotics competitions are among the most well known of their kind. Their website has information about challenges, contests and other opportunities.

IEEE Robotics and Automation Society
445 Hoes Lane
Piscataway, NJ 08854
Phone: (732) 562-3906

Website: http://www.ieee-ras.org

Twitter: @ieeeras

The Robotics and Automation Society is part of the Institute of Electrical and Electronic Engineers (IEEE). It focuses on advancing innovation, education and research in robotics and automation.

The Robotics Alliance Project

National Aeronautics and Space
Administration (NASA)
NASA Headquarters
300 E Street SW
Washington, DC 20546-0001
Phone: (202) 358-0001

Website: http://robotics.nasa.gov

Twitter: @NASA_RAP

A branch of NASA, the Robotics Alliance
Project focuses on getting students
interested in and prepared for careers in
the space industry dealing with robotics.

The Robotics Institute

Carnegie Mellon University
5000 Forbes Avenue
Pittsburgh, PA 15213-3890
Phone: (412) 268-3818

Website: http://www.ri.cmu.edu/index.html

The Robotics Institute at Carnegie Mellon
University offers programs for students
interested in working in robotics.

Cassriel, Betsy. *Robot Builders!* Broomall, PA: Mason Crest Publishers, 2015.

Cook, David. *Robot Building for Beginners*. Berkeley, CA: Apress, 2015.

Hulick, Kathryn. *Careers in Robotics* San Diego, CA: ReferencePoint Press, 2017.

Hulick, Kathryn. *How Robotics Is Changing the World*. San Diego, CA: ReferencePoint Press, 2019.

Hustad, Douglas. *Discover Robotics*. Minneapolis, MN: Lerner Publications, 2017.

Lacey, Saskia. *STEM Careers: Reinventing Robotics*. Huntington Beach, CA: Teacher Created Materials, 2017.

Mara, Wil. *Robotics Engineers*. Ann Arbor, MI: Cherry Lake Publishing, 2015.

Nardo, Don. *How Robotics Is Changing Society*. San Diego, CA: ReferencePoint Press, 2016.

Peppas, Lynn. *Robotics*. New York, NY: Crabtree Publishing, 2015.

Salemi, Behnam. *Robot Building for Teens*. Boston, MA: Cengage Learning, 2015.

Spilsbury, Louise, and Richard Spilsbury. *Robotics*. New York, NY: Gareth Stevens Publishing, 2017.

Index